C++ PROGRAMMING GUIDELINES

Thomas Plum
Dan Saks

Plum Hall Inc

Acknowledgement of trademarks: Instant-C is a trademark of Rational Systems; MS-DOS is a trademark of Microsoft; UNIX is a trademark of AT&T; C++ is not a trademark.

Printed in the United States of America.

ISBN 0-911537-10-4

10 9 8 7 6 5 4 3 2 1

For Lana and Nancy

PREFACE

As with C, there are three primary reasons why programming projects adopt coding standards for C++:

Reliability: Each program should produce a predictable, correct behavior.

Readability/Maintainability: Clarity and consistency assist maintainers in making revisions properly.

Portability: People expect to be able to move applications to new hardware and new compilers.

In addition, the process of migrating an organization from C to C++ provides new challenges for making project guidelines. The guidelines herein address these issues of migration and compatibility.

We are attempting to provide guidelines for the wide variety of ways that C++ is used. This is challenging, because C++ covers an even wider domain of applicability than does C: C++ is now (or will soon be) available as an alternative to C for the lowest-level firmware and embedded-systems work, and yet provides strong support for "programming-in-the-large". Some guidelines for "programming-in-the-large" add a few more lines of code than the most abbreviated style. We think that our readers are more interested in large systems that work reliably than in the most compact coding examples.

Our guiding principle throughout is that good programming guidelines are based upon the cognitive intuition of the programmers that use them. Avoiding "surprises" is the key to reliable use of a programming language; a powerful, subtle, sophisticated technique that works ninety-five percent of the time is inappropriate for general use on a software project. Just as with C, successful C++ programmers impose restrictions upon their usage of the language, in order to work within that subset known to them and their project to give predictable, reliable results. Our goal herein is to make some of those experience-based restrictions explicit, to describe the reasons for them, and to discuss some of the tradeoffs associated with them.

We have both worked to make C and C++ available not just to veteran programmers but also to professionals who have an *application* expertise. Among Plum Hall's clientele have been doctors, engineers, lawyers, and off-Broadway directors, all of whom shared a need to convert their application knowledge into working programs. This book is a continuation of our efforts to make real programming power accessible to the widest audience that can effectively use it.

We particularly focus upon projects which are migrating from C to C++, especially those projects that are familiar with the Plum Hall *C Programming Guidelines*. This book incorporates all of those C guidelines which are still relevant to C++, and discusses the reasons for discontinuing others. These C topics appear at the end of each chapter. A new Chapter 5 collects all the lexical rules. (However, the 60-page detailed discussion of ANSI/ISO Standard C is not incorporated in this book.)

Plum Hall also provides these Guidelines in machine-readable form for projects wishing to incorporate this material into their local programming standard.

For their thoughtful comments on various of the versions of this material, we are grateful to James Abbott, Mike Ball, Tom Bannon, Lucy Berlin, Ann Bertrand, Mark Boggs, Dennis Brandl, John Cannon, Don Caraway, John Carolan, Terry Caudill, Allen Chambers, Rick Christiansen, Bruce Eckel, Andy Fergenson, Mary Fontana, Neal Gafter, Charles Gardner, Don Hardcastle, David Hearn, Phil Housley, Shawn Islam, John Jensen, Carey Jung, Brian Kennedy, Joan Lee, Mark Linton, Dane Meyer, Mike Miller, Ron Mitchell, Chuck Muraski, Jill Nail, Dwight Neal, Martin Neath, Ron Patton, Glen Peace, Bob Peterson, P. J. Plauger, Mike Prather, Roland Racko, Fred Raines, Mark Ramey, Mike Reynolds, Paul Schmidt, Russ Schnall, Christopher Skelly, Diana Sparacin, Richard Smith, Henry Tieding, Frank Vretos, Brian Victor, Sean Vikören, Ed Wells, Frank Yen.

Thomas Plum   Dan Saks

Plum Hall Inc   Saks and Associates
609-927-3770   513-324-3601
plum@plumhall.com

CONTENTS

CHAPTER 0	INTRODUCTION	
0.01 standards	standards and guidelines	11
0.02 levels	levels of use	12
0.03 design	which design methods to use	16
0.04 de-facto	de-facto standard for C++	18

CHAPTER 1	DATA AND VARIABLES	
1.01 ADT	abstract data type	20
1.02 struct	just-a-struct	24
1.03 effects	effects of constructors and destructors	26
1.04 name	global name conflicts	28
1.05 nullptr	null pointer constant	30
1.06 refs	use of references	32
1.07 memory	pointer into object	36
1.08 dangling	dangling references	38
1.09 nested	nested types	40
1.10 init	object declaration and initialization	44
1.11 const	concrete const vs. abstract const	48
1.12 constfn	const member functions	52
1.13 friend	friend functions	54
1.14 static	static data members	58
1.15 paramtypes	parameterized types	60
1.16 names	choosing variable names	64
1.17 stdtypes	standard defined-types	68
1.18 constants	maintainability of constants	70
1.19 wordlen	word and byte size	72
1.20 byteorder	byte ordering	74
1.21 charconsts	character constants	76
1.22 ptrtypes	pointer types	78
1.23 ptrconv	pointer conversions	80
1.24 alloc	allocation integrity	82
1.25 structs	structures	84
1.26 strings	string literals	86

C++ PROGRAMMING GUIDELINES

CHAPTER 2	OPERATORS	
2.01 temp	dynamics of temporaries	88
2.02 overload	managing overloading	90
2.03 newdel	overloading new and delete	98
2.04 casts	keep casts significant	100
2.05 cast	casting objects	102
2.06 evalorder	allowable dependencies on evaluation order	104
2.07 parens	parentheses	106
2.08 rightshift	right-shift and unsigned data	108
2.09 sideorder	order of side effects	110
2.10 conv	conversions and overflow	112
2.11 ctype	character tests	114
CHAPTER 3	CONTROL STATEMENTS	
3.01 loopscope	scope of loop variable	116
3.02 while	while	118
3.03 loopinvar	designing with loop invariants	120
3.04 elseif	multiple-choice constructs	124
3.05 control	restrictions on control structures	126
3.06 structure	program structure and problem structure	128
CHAPTER 4	FUNCTIONS AND OTHER MODULES	
4.01 codemgt	code management	130
4.02 const	referencing unmodified arguments	134
4.03 defarg	default arguments	136
4.04 globinit	initialization of global objects	138
4.05 preproc	minimizing use of preprocessor	140
4.06 headers	project-wide standard headers	144
4.07 files	size of source files	146
4.08 includes	put includes at head of file	148
4.09 stdflags	standard compile-time flags	150
4.10 nest	nested headers	152
4.11 noinit	no initializations in headers	154
4.12 coupling	methods of coupling modules together	156
4.13 cohesion	cohesion and meaningful functions	158
4.14 libfns	file structure for procedural library functions	160
4.15 portlib	use of portable library	162
4.16 fnsize	suggested size of functions	164
4.17 macros	writing macros	166
4.18 stdarg	functions of a variable number of arguments	168
4.19 ptrparms	pointer and reference parameters	170
4.20 headers	contents of local standard headers	172

CHAPTER 5	LEXICAL LAYOUT RULES	
5.01 lexdata	lexical rules for variables	176
5.02 lexops	lexical rules for operators	178
5.03 lexctl	lexical rules for control structure	180
5.04 lexfns	lexical rules for functions	186

CHAPTER 6	GENERAL STANDARDS	
6.01 pragmatics	architectural issues in code re-use	188
6.02 errors	error-handling	192
6.03 port	portability and intentional non-portability	196
6.04 measure	measuring productivity of code re-use	198
6.05 effic	efficiency	200
6.06 virtual_fct	virtual functions	204
6.07 virtual_dtor	virtual destructors	208
6.08 base_class	avoiding changes to derived classes	210
6.09 protected	protected members	212
6.10 firewalls	compilation firewalls	214
6.11 comments	suggested use of comments	218
6.12 specs	specifications	220
6.13 reviews	code reviews	222
6.14 defensive	defensive programming	224
6.15 simplicity	simplicity of design and implementation	226

CHAPTER 7	VERSIONS OF C++	
7.01 versions	versions of C++	228
7.02 C_problems	problem areas from C	232
7.03 when	when to use C, when to use C++	234
7.04 TypesafeC	the intersection of Standard C and C++	236
7.05 mixing	mixing C and C++ code	240
7.06 paramtypes	parameterized types	242

CHAPTER 8	APPENDICES	
8.01 review	first-order correctness review and test	244
8.02 benches	simple benchmark programs	250
8.03 bib	bibliography	260

CHAPTER 9	INDEX	263

TOPIC: 0.01 standards - standards and guidelines

STANDARD

Criteria labeled as "STANDARD" are mandatory for all code included in a product.

The need for exceptions may occasionally arise, but the exception requires a specific justification, and the justification should be documented with the source code. This is a "permissive" approach to exceptions; this book is not intended by itself to satisfy any legal, auditing, or quality-assurance criteria.

Project-wide exceptions to the standards may be justified and should be documented as an appendix to the standard.

Criteria labeled as "GUIDELINE" are recommended practices. Experience has shown that differing approaches can coexist in these areas. It is expected that, in general, a majority of programmers will follow the guidelines, so that they represent a widely-accepted pattern.

TOPIC: 0.02 levels - levels of use

GUIDELINE

Projects may elect to use all, or only a subset, of the C++ language. There are at least three different levels of use for C++:

1.   "Typesafe C", the common subset of Standard C and C++,

2.   "Object-Based C++", C++ using classes but not derivation, and

3.   "Full C++", the entire C++ language.

Projects should use Typesafe C when some of the target platform(s) and development environment support Standard C, not C++, and the developers plan to migrate the project to C++ or to integrate part of it with other (current or future) C++ projects. These circumstances include the case where there is only one target platform, and it only supports C. This implies that all software projects using C should use Typesafe C. (See Section 7.04.)

Projects should move beyond Typesafe C when they are ready to use classes to implement abstract data types (Section 1.01, ADTs.). Projects with a commitment to using object-oriented techniques should use the entire C++ language. However, projects may also elect to use only object-based techniques and restrict their use of C++ accordingly. Note here the distinction between *object-based* and *object-oriented* techniques (Wegner, 1990). Object-based programming includes data abstraction (classes) and encapsulation (access control), but not inheritance (class derivation) and polymorphism (virtual functions). Object-oriented programming encompasses all of these techniques.

Object-Based C++ includes language features that support convenient and efficient object-based programming, such as function name and operator overloading, inline functions, friend functions and references. Where available, it also includes templates and exception handling.

Projects should restrict themselves to using Object-Based C++ when:

1.   The project developers understand object-based techniques, and the project does not have the resources to develop fully-reliable methodologies for object-oriented techniques.

2.   The project designers determine that object-oriented techniques are not appropriate for that task at hand.

JUSTIFICATION

Making the transition from C to C++ poses strategic as well as technical problems. Introducing new languages and methodologies, such as C++ and object-oriented design, helps organizations maintain a competitive advantage, but too much innovation all at once can be risky. Approaching C++ through progressive levels reduces those risks.

There is mounting evidence that the transition from C to C++ and from procedural to object-oriented designs takes time and experience. Software managers should encourage and assist developers in moving to higher levels of use, but not institute methodology for general use until experience shows that their staff can use that methodology reliably. Projects should progress through the levels of use at a rate appropriate to the background of the staff.

Programming in Typesafe C lets programmers adapt to new C++ development tools and stricter type checking, without compelling a change in design methodologies. Typesafe C programming imposes no practical restrictions on the expressive power of C. It provides seamless integration of C software into C++ projects without abandoning those platforms that do not support C++.

Projects should resist the temptation to abandon Typesafe C just to use C++ as a "Better C", that is, to use features such as operator overloading, references and inline functions, but not classes. By providing language-level support for abstraction and encapsulation, classes offer clear reasons to abandon compatibility with C. While the "Better C" features may enhance the power of object-based and object-oriented programming in C++, by themselves these features do not provide sufficient reason to abandon the portability and stability of C.

Object-Based C++ provides programmers with the opportunity to learn and apply data abstraction and encapsulation techniques without making a complete "paradigm shift" to object-oriented design and programming. Languages such as Ada and Modula-2 support object-based programming, but not object-oriented programming. C programmers with additional experience in one of these languages will find Object-Based C++ easy to learn. Projects have identified gains in productivity from working at this level (Mancl, 1989).

ALTERNATIVES

Projects may identify intermediate levels between 1 and 2. One possibility is to allow application programmers to use classes, but not implement their own. At this level, programmers must be trained to use a limited number of C++ features, such as constructors, member function calls, and references. They must also be alerted to potential pitfalls, such as the implementation-dependent lifetime of temporaries.

Another alternative is to adopt Object-Based C++ as the method for general use, but provide inheritance-based class libraries written by a more experienced group. Documentation for such libraries must include guidelines sufficient to ensure that constructors, destructors, and member functions perform without surprises. (See Chapter 6 for specific guidelines.)

[LOCAL NOTES]

[LOCAL NOTES]

TOPIC: 0.03 design - which design methods to use

GUIDELINE

There are a variety of design approaches:

     System-oriented: focuses upon *subsystems*, i.e. *class categories*.

     Object-oriented: focuses upon *classes*.

     Dataflow-oriented: focuses upon *processes*.

     Hierarchy-oriented: focuses upon *modules*.

     Procedure-oriented: focuses upon *algorithms*.

     State-oriented: focuses upon *state transitions*.

     Rule-oriented: focuses upon *goals*.

     Constraint-oriented: focuses upon *invariants*.

Each of these design approaches may be productive for some portion of an overall project. The most "macro" (top-level) of them may be the system-oriented design level, characterized by the slogan "Real systems have no top".

The continual challenge facing us, as managers, designers, and programmers, is to determine which methods, or sets of methods, are most appropriate to the real-life problems that we are presented with.

During the early 1990's, most programming projects will benefit from incorporating the object-oriented design approach into their repertoire of techniques. C++ is, of course, excellently suited for the implementation of object-oriented designs, but its applicability is not restricted to object-oriented designs. C++ is a fully general-purpose programming language, suitable to the efficient implementation of all of the design approaches.

Within the general category of object-oriented design, it is worthwhile to distinguish two subcategories:

     Inheritance-based: focuses upon *inheritance* hierarchies.

     Object-based: focuses upon *encapsulation*, the grouping of state and behavior into classes, without much use of inheritance.

The full expressive power of C++ is in inheritance-based usage, but many of the programming "surprises" are also found at this level. This fact affects several of the Guidelines herein.

REFERENCES

Grady Booch, Object-Oriented Design, 1991.

See Section 8.03, Bibliography, for all reference details.

[LOCAL NOTES]

TOPIC: 0.04 de-facto - de-facto standard for C++

GUIDELINE

When deciding which features of C++ to assume for future project
environments, Ellis & Stroustrup's *Annotated C++ Reference Manual*
(1990) is the de-facto standard. A version of this book was adopted as
a base document for X3J16, the ANSI C++ standardization committee.
It is likely that X3J16 will produce a standard fairly close to the
language described in E&S (1990).

Until all your target environments support this version of C++, see
Chapter 7 for further guidelines about handling the interim transition.

[LOCAL NOTES]

[LOCAL NOTES]

TOPIC: 1.01 ADT - abstract data type

GUIDELINE

An abstract data type (ADT) is a data type whose client interface and functional specification are completely separate from its implementation. An ADT should not allow client code to inspect or modify its representation except through public member or friend functions that define the client interface with the ADT. An ADT is also known as an *encapsulated data type*. When programming in Object-Based C++ or Full C++, implement each ADT as a class (using the keyword `class` and not `struct`).

An ADT's interface generally consists of the following types of functions (Gorlen, et. al., 1990 and Lippman, 1989):

1. *manager functions*, such constructors, destructors, assignment operators and type conversion operators,

2. *implementor functions* that define the permissible operations on and modifications to an object, and

3. *accessor functions* that return information about the state of an object.

The interface may include other classes, such as an iterator for the ADT, which should be nested if possible (Section 1.09). It may also include types and constants, preferably nested.

Do not declare public member data or public static data in an ADT. Rather, provide accessor functions to permit client code to inspect the attributes of an ADT object. Define mutator functions (a special case of implementors) to let clients alter the attributes of an ADT object. (A mutator modifies a single attribute, as opposed to an implementor that may operate on the entire state of the object.) Accessors and mutators are also known as "get" and "set" functions. For a given attribute of an ADT, the accessor and mutator should have the same name (similar, but not identical, to the data member's name).

An accessor is a `const` member function with an empty argument list that returns the value of the attribute. An accessor may return a `const` reference to the attribute to avoid unnecessary temporaries or copying, but it should never return a non-`const` pointer or reference to class member data.

A mutator is a non-`const` member function that uses one or more argument values to modify the value of an attribute. A mutator should return the new value of the attribute, an integral value indicating the

    Copyright © 1991, Thomas Plum and Dan Saks

success of the mutation, or `void`.

EXAMPLE

```
class bad_ADT
    {
public:
    attr_type attribute;                            // BAD - public data
    // ...
    };

class ADT
    {
public:
    attr_type attr() const { return attribute; }   // accessor
    void attr(attr_type a) { attribute = a; }       // mutator
    // ...
private:
    // ...
    attr_type attribute;                            // private data
    };
```

GUIDELINE

Do not define a default constructor, copy constructor, assignment
operator or destructor for a class unless there is a functional reason to
override the default functions generated by the compiler. However,
every class representing an ADT that does not define these member
functions should document that the generated versions of the functions
provide the intended functionality. And if any form of constructor is
provided, you must also provide a default constructor.

Carroll (1990) advises that input and output operations on an object of
an ADT should preserve the object's value. He provides this example:

```
T oldt = v;
Pipestream p;
p << oldt;              // put object to Pipestream
T newt;
p >> newt;              // get object from Pipestream
assert(oldt == newt);   // == is T.operator==()
```

The assertion should be true.

The following guidelines contribute to reliable use of member functions:

Provide explicit bounds-checking in the function interface.

21

Keep data in a consistent state.

Make explicit provision for the possibility of overflow.

Keep all data (files, tables, windows, etc.) in a consistent state.

Provide access to useful subfunctions that are used in each package.

JUSTIFICATION

By definition, an ADT's interface should completely hide its implementation. Providing public member data gives clients direct access to the implementation and violates that abstraction. Accessors and mutators that return a non-const pointer or reference to class member data are equivalent to providing public member data.

Construction, destruction and assignment are fundamental operations for most ADTs. The compiler generates them if they are omitted from a class, but the generated versions don't always provide behavior that's appropriate for a class.

Requiring that all ADTs always define a default constructor, copy constructor and destructor may increase the code and execution time of programs (Section 6.05). Also, unless the user-defined copy constructor and assignment operator have the exact same prototypes as the generated functions, some C++ compilers will still create a generated copy constructor or assignment. This can cause bugs that are hard to find.

ALTERNATIVES

The names of accessors and mutators should always begin with get and set, respectively. For an attribute stored in private data member attr, the accessor would be getAttr() or get_attr(), and the mutator would be setAttr() or set_attr().

GUIDELINE

When writing in Typesafe C, implement an ADT as a struct whose type name is typedef'ed to its tag name, such as

```
typedef struct complex complex;
```
Provide a complete set of functions or function-like macros that define the ADT's functionality, so that clients need not directly manipulate fields of the ADT.

EXAMPLE

The FILE structure is a familiar example of a C struct implementing an ADT:

```
struct FILE
    {
    char *_cur_ptr; /* where to get/put the next character; !0 */
    int  _size;     /* how big is the buffer: {0:INT_MAX} */
    char *_buffer;  /* where is the buffer: char [_size] | 0 */
    int  _rcount;   /* how many more gets left: {0:_size} */
    int  _wcount;   /* how many more puts left: {0:_size} */
    char _status;   /* file state: bits */
    char _fd;       /* file descriptor: {0:_NFILES-1} */
    };
typedef struct FILE FILE;
```

At higher levels of C++ use, it would be implemented as a class (presumably named File instead of FILE). But the encapsulation technique is familiar to C programmers — clients manipulate FILE structures only through library functions and library macros.

ALTERNATIVES

Prefix each member name with an underscore. This is common practice for ADT's in the Standard C library, as in the example above. This practice provides a convenient rule of thumb to detect violations of the encapsulation of an ADT, namely, no client code may directly access any field whose name begins with an underscore.

[LOCAL NOTES]

23

TOPIC: 1.02 struct - just-a-struct

GUIDELINE

In contrast to an ADT, project programs may sometimes use "just-a-struct". Data elements that are gathered into just-a-struct may be inspected or changed just like scalar variables.

Regardless of the level of C++ use, always refer to a variable that is just-a-struct using the keyword `struct`, such as "struct time_day". In just-a-struct, none of the member names should have leading underscores.

EXAMPLE

The following structure might be used by a low-level hardware interface function to directly access a 32-bit timer interface:

```
/* time_day.h - bit-field structure for  hh:mm:ss.fff */
struct time_day
    {
    unsigned h1 : 2;     /* tens digit of hours        : (0:2) */
    unsigned h2 : 4;     /* units digit of hours       : (0:9) */
    unsigned m1 : 3;     /* tens digit of minutes      : (0:5) */
    unsigned m2 : 4;     /* units digit of minutes     : (0:9) */
    unsigned s1 : 3;     /* tens digit of seconds      : (0:5) */
    unsigned s2 : 4;     /* units digit of seconds     : (0:9) */
    unsigned f1 : 4;     /* first digit of fraction    : (0:9) */
    unsigned f2 : 4;     /* second digit of fraction   : (0:9) */
    unsigned f3 : 4;     /* third digit of fraction    : (0:9) */
    };       /* 32 bits total */

    /* ... */
struct time_day t1, t2;     /* OK - "struct" means just-a-struct */
    /* ... */
t1.f1 = t1.f2 = t1.f3 = 0;  /* OK - accessible members */
```

JUSTIFICATION

There is such a thing as excess generality. When just-a-struct is adequate, encapsulating it just introduces complication.

[LOCAL NOTES]

[LOCAL NOTES]

TOPIC: 1.03 effects - effects of constructors and destructors

GUIDELINE

Use constructors to initialize objects. That initialization may, and often does, include allocating resources, such as memory or files.

Use destructors to destroy the values of objects. A destructor typically releases resources used by an object. Constructors and destructors may modify static data members used for resource management, performance analysis, or debugging; they should have no other external side-effects.

Use static member initializers to initialize static data members. Do not initialize static data members within a constructor, except to avoid depending on the order of static initialization (Section 4.04). For example,

```
class X
    {
    static int count;
public:
    X()
        {
        count = 0;      // BAD - initializing static member
                        //       in constructor
        }
    };

int X::count = 0;       // OK - use static initializer
```

Unless a class is explicitly defined to perform input or output, its constructors and destructors should not accept input or generate output except within conditionally-compiled diagnostic statements.

JUSTIFICATION

As a general rule, all functions should avoid side-effects seemingly unrelated to the task at hand. Side-effects generally increase the complexity of systems by increasing the coupling between components. Constructors and destructors are intended to create and destroy values of objects, and should do no more.

Static data members store information common to all objects of a class. Static data should be initialized prior to the construction of the first object of the class. If a constructor initializes static data, that data will be reinitialized every time a new object is created. The constructor can avoid reinitialization by using a counter, but then the counter must have a static initializer.

ALTERNATIVES

Some older implementations of C++ prohibit general expressions in static initializers. If a static data member's initializing expression is too complicated for static initialization, initialize that member inside a constructor. Use the same technique used to avoid order dependencies in static initializers (Section 4.04).

[LOCAL NOTES]

TOPIC: 1.04 name - global name conflicts

GUIDELINE

Name conflicts can occur when separately developed software components use the same identifier but for different purposes. For example, if two libraries each provide a global function foo with the same signature, a program that uses both libraries may encounter link errors reporting that a function with foo in the signature is multiply defined. No program can call both versions of foo.

Avoid global name conflicts by avoiding global names:

1.   Use member functions instead of global friend functions and non-member functions (Section 1.13).

2.   Use static member data instead of global non-member data (Section 1.14).

3.   Whenever non-member function and data names must be at file scope, use the static storage-class specifier to restrict linkage to that one file.

4.   Avoid macros. Use inline functions (preferably members), enumerations, and const declarations (Section 4.05).

5.   Use nested types where appropriate (Section 1.09).

Use a project-wide or vendor-wide prefix for each remaining global name in a reusable component library. Longer prefixes reduce likelihood of clashes with other prefixes. Use local consts and typedefs to define shorter, more convenient aliases for internal use. The aliases may be distributed with the reusable components, but use of the aliases must be optional and reconfigurable.

Each use of scope-resolution :: should raise a question: why is this necessary here?

JUSTIFICATION

Even nested classes cannot eliminate all global type names. Global classes are an important by-product of object-based and object-oriented programming in C++. Projects must pursue policies for sharing software components without fear of global name conflicts.

ALTERNATIVES

The following technique for avoiding name conflicts is based on work by Linton, et. al. for the *InterViews 3.0* library. The technique uses a macro to rename global identifiers with a unique project-wide prefix. Other macros provide shorter aliases for convenient use.

The Interviews header(s) defines a prefixing macro

```
#define iv(Name) iv##Name
```

Also, for each global name, Name, the header(s) define a renaming macro

```
#define Name iv(Name)
```

For example, the Interviews source uses the name Interactor, which actually expands (through two macro calls) to ivInteractor. Another Interviews header file #undef's all the renaming macros.

A source file effectively "enters" the InterViews naming scope by #include'ing one file, and "leaves" by #include'ing another. For example, suppose another library also has class called Interactor. If a given source file only uses InterViews Interactor or the other library's Interactor, no special action is necessary because the linker sees Interactor and ivInteractor as distinct names. On the other hand, for a single source file to use the Interactors from both libraries, it must contain code like:

```
#include <other-interactor.h>

#include <InterViews/interactor.h>
#include <interViews/leave_scope.h>

// use iv(Interactor) for InterViews and ...
// use Interactor for the other library
```

[LOCAL NOTES]

TOPIC: 1.05 nullptr - null pointer constant

STANDARD

Use the integer constant zero (0) as the null pointer constant for both data and function pointers. Do not use a cast.

Cast 0 to an appropriate pointer type when passing a null pointer constant as an unchecked argument of a variable-length argument list function. (In general, avoid variable-length argument lists because the arguments are not checked for type correctness.)

Do not use the macro NULL.

JUSTIFICATION

A constant expression that evaluates to 0 is converted to a pointer, commonly called the null pointer, whenever it is assigned, compared or used to initialize a pointer. Using 0 as null is consistent with common usage in published C++ texts. This notation is both compact and portable.

The conversion to pointer is not performed when passing 0 as an unchecked argument, so this special case requires a cast.

E&S (1990) does not guarantee that the defined constant NULL is compatible with all pointer types. Some implementations define NULL as (void *)0, which cannot be assigned to another pointer type without a cast. The symbol NULL is actually an artifact of old C. Before C had prototypes, NULL was needed to assure that null pointer arguments had the correct size.

EXAMPLE

```
char *p = NULL; /* BAD - may give "syntax error"! */
                /* if NULL defined as (void*)0 */

char *p = 0;    /* OK - uses integer 0 without a cast */

printf("null looks like %p\n", (void *)0);
                /* OK - uses (cast)0 for unchecked arg */
```

ALTERNATIVES

Programmers migrating from C may prefer to continue using NULL. However, it may be necessary to modify some vendor headers to insure that NULL is always zero, and not (void *)0. In any event, it is still necessary to cast NULL to the appropriate type when passed as an unchecked argument.

[LOCAL NOTES]

TOPIC: 1.06 refs - use of references

GUIDELINE

References may be used as function parameters and return types. References can be used to pass objects to be altered by a function, as in:

```
void manipulate(object &obj);        // OK - can modify object
```

Use a const reference as an efficient alternative to passing a copy of an object:

```
void lookat(const bigobject &big);   // OK - avoids passing by value
```

References are often preferable to pointers for these uses, because references carry a stronger semantic guarantee — a reference remains bound to an object for the lifetime of the reference, whereas a pointer can change.

Common examples for the usefulness of references are copy constructors and default assignment operators:

```
X::X(const X &);              // copy constructor
X &X::operator=(const X &);   // assignment operator
```

In general, member and friend function of a class should not return a reference to an object that is part of the internal representation of that class. Rather, use implementor, accessor or mutator functions to inspect of modify the internals of the object (Section 1.01).

There are exceptions to this guideline that must be handled thoughtfully. For example, container classes such as strings and vectors may define operator[] to return a reference to an element in the container. Also, a "smart pointer" class may define unary operator* to return a reference to the object addressed by the smart pointer. However, users should avoid binding the return value from such a function to a named reference whose lifetime outlasts the lifetime of the referenced object. The class developer must document the rules for safe use of references returned by member and friend functions.

References may be used as class members and as ordinary variables. As with parameters, they provide a stronger semantic guarantee of invariance. Such use is, however, subject to the necessary analysis to prevent dangling pointers and references (Section 1.08.)

EXAMPLE

For a class of vector of integers, operator[] may be declared to return a reference to a vector element, as

```
int &Vector::Vector operator[](size_t);
```
Returning a reference enables the result to be used as an lvalue, as in
```
Vector v(20);
// ...
v[i] = k;
```
Users should be extremely cautious about saving references to elements of a vector. For example, assignment to a vector may return the vector elements to the free store and allocate new elements. Some of the following operations may be dangerous:
```
Vector v1(20), v2(30);
// ...

v2[i] = v1[i];      // OK - reference used only momentarily
// ...

int &r = v1[i];     // BAD - reference to element may disappear
v1 = v2;            // assignment may deallocate v1's old elements
r = 3;              // BAD - assignment through dangling reference
```

JUSTIFICATION

The overhead of using a reference is typically about the same as that of a pointer, with any optimization possibility typically favoring the reference. The compiler knows that the address held in the reference will be constant during the reference's lifetime.

Indeed, the semantics of a reference can be defined like this: Replace the reference declarator &x with a pointer declarator *const px. Replace each initialization (including argument-passing) expression y with its address &y. Replace every occurrence of the reference variable x with *px:
```
/* reference version */       /* equivalent semantics with pointer */
int & x  = y;                 int *const px  = &y;

if (x == 1)                   if (*px == 1)
    f(x + 1);                     f(*px + 1);
```

These examples can be verbalized more fluently if the reference symbol & is spoken aloud as "ref".

Functions that return references to objects in the internal representation of a class cannot be used safely without some knowledge of the internals of that class. Class implementors should avoid defining such functions, or document rules for safe usage.

The exact point of destruction for temporaries is version-dependent. References to the internal representation of temporary objects can easily become dangling references.

[LOCAL NOTES]

[LOCAL NOTES]

TOPIC: 1.07 memory - pointer into object

GUIDELINE

In general, member and friend functions of a class should not return a pointer to an object that is part of the internal representation of that class. For a container class such as a list or vector that holds pointers, the pointers are considered to be values in the container and not part of the internal representation of the container.

There are exceptions to this guideline that must be handled thoughtfully. It is widespread practice to implement conversion operators like

```
String::operator char*();   // warning - points inside String
```

that returns a pointer to the internal representation of a `String`. In some applications, this operator could produce a dangling pointer (see Section 2.01). Alternatively, this operator could be defined to return a pointer to a newly allocated copy of the string's text, but this could cause memory leaks (failure to return storage to the free store).

The class developer must document the rules for safe use of pointers returned by member and friend functions.

This guideline should not be construed to discourage the implementation of "smart pointer" classes. In such a class `P`, the member function `P::operator->` returns a pointer that is a data member of `P`, not a pointer to the internals of `P`.

EXAMPLE

In a class for a stack of elements of type `T`, a function `top` that returns the value at the top of the stack (non-destructively) should be declared as

```
T Stack::top();          // OK - returns copy of top element
```
and not as
```
T *Stack::top();         // BAD - returns pointer to top element
```

JUSTIFICATION

Functions that return pointers into the internals of objects cannot be used safely without some knowledge of the inner workings of that class. This violates the encapsulation of the class.

The exact point of destruction for temporaries is version-dependent. (See Section 2.01.)

[LOCAL NOTES]

[LOCAL NOTES]

TOPIC: 1.08 dangling – dangling references

STANDARD

Do not initialize a reference to refer to the object whose address is the null pointer. For example,

```
int *p = 0;
int &r = *p;        // BAD - r is a null reference
// ...
r = 4;              // BAD - assignment through null
```

Do not bind a reference to an object in the free store that might be deleted via a pointer. For example,

```
T *p = new T;
T &r = *p;          // BAD - ref to delete-able object
// ...
delete p;
r = T(4);           // BAD - assignment to deleted object
```

A function should not return a reference to an object whose lifetime ends upon return from that function. Such objects include the actual arguments of the function and automatic variables declared in that function.

JUSTIFICATION

A reference to an object of type T must be initialized by an object that is, or is convertible to, type T; however, the null pointer doesn't point to an object.

Returning a reference to automatic storage whose lifetime has ended is similar to returning a pointer to such storage. Both actions produce undefined behavior.

EXAMPLE

```
int &foo(int &i)
   {
   int j;
   // ...
   return i;        // OK - referenced object survives return
   // ...
   return j;        // BAD - j deallocated by return from foo
   }
```

```
X &X::bar(X &xr, X y)
    {
    // ...
    return xr;        // OK - referenced object survives return
    // ...
    return y;         // BAD - y destroyed by return from bar
    // ...
    return *this;     // OK - referenced object survives return
    }
```

[LOCAL NOTES]

TOPIC: 1.09 nested - nested types

GUIDELINE

Use nested types to reduce global name conflicts.

EXAMPLE

Linked data structures, like lists and trees, commonly use names like node for the class of objects referenced by links. However, most linked structures need a unique node type. Nesting each node class inside the definition of its corresponding linked data structure avoids name conflicts when using more than one linked data structure in a single program.

```
class list
    {
public:
    list();
    // ...
private:
    struct node        // OK - nested struct localizes type name
        {
        sometype value;
        node *next;
        };
    node *first;
    };
```

JUSTIFICATION

In addition to avoiding global name conflicts, nested types describe *has-a* relationships more clearly than non-nested friend classes (see ALTERNATIVE below). For example, nesting struct node inside class list in the example above clearly establishes that nodes are part of lists.

GUIDELINE

Use nested public classes to implement uniform naming schemes for closely related types.

EXAMPLE

Container classes (such as list or set) with iterators can uniformly use iterator as the iterator class name if the iterator class definition is nested inside the container class definition.

Copyright © 1991, Thomas Plum and Dan Saks

```
class list
    {
public:
    list();
    // ...
    class iterator  // OK - nested iterator class
        {
    public:
        iterator(const list &);
        // ...
    private:
        // ...
        };
private:
    // ...
    };

list my_list;
list::iterator i(my_list);
                // OK - unique reference to nested type
```

ALTERNATIVES

E&S (1990) changed the scope rules for nested types. Earlier versions of C++ export nested types to the scope of the enclosing class. The guidelines and examples above assume that C++ compilers support the proper nesting of types as described by E&S.

When programming for C++ compilers that do not support the newer scope rules, do not use lexically nested types. That is, do not declare a type name (class, struct, enum, union or typedef) inside another class (class, struct or union) definition. Prefix the names of the "nested" types with the name of the "enclosing" class. For example, if class node should (but can't) be nested in class tree, then declare node as a non-nested class tree_node.

If "nested" class x_y should only be accessed by "enclosing" class x, declare x as a friend of x_y and declare all members of x_y, including

41

the constructors, as either private or protected.

EXAMPLE

```
class list_node      // OK - non-nested class with...
    {
    friend class list;                  // friend class and...
    list_node(const sometype &v, list_node *p)
        : value(v), next(p) {}          // private constructor
    sometype value;
    list_node *next;
    };

class list          // OK - friend class
    {
public:
    list();
    // ...
private:
    list_node *first;
    };
```

[LOCAL NOTES]

[LOCAL NOTES]

TOPIC: 1.10 init - object declaration and initialization

GUIDELINE

Use an explicit initializer when declaring an automatic or register object. Avoid using the default constructor followed by a later assignment. That is, any of

```
T x (i);
T x = i;
T x = T(i);
```

are typically preferred to

```
T x;
// ...
x = i;
```

This preference also applies to declarations of local static objects when the initializer is a constant expression.

This guideline implies that automatic and register objects should be declared at the point of first use rather than at the beginning of the enclosing block. For example,

```
String bye;            // BAD - wasted call on constructor
// ...
String hi = "hello";   // OK - hi declared just before use
for (i = 0; i < hi.length(); ++i)
    // ...
bye = "goodbye";
```

Use the forms

```
T x = i;
T x = T(i);
```

when the initializer i is the initial value of the object, and use the form

```
T x (i);
```

when the initializer represents an initial size or dimension. For example,

```
complex c1 = 1;            // c1 = 1 + 0i;
complex c2 = complex(2, -3);   // c2 = 2 - 3i;
vector v (20);             // v has 20 elements
```

Don't combine default initialization followed by assignment into a single explicit initialization when the argument of the constructor has a different meaning from the argument of the assignment. For example, a vector class may be implemented so that

```
Vector v;
```
creates a vector with a default dimension and
```
Vector v (20);
```
creates a vector with 20 elements. However,
```
v = 20;
```
may assign the value 20 to every element of v. In this case, don't replace
```
Vector v;
// ...
v = 20;
```
with
```
Vector v (20);
```
It might also be necessary to keep default initialization and assignment separate for static objects. When the initializer i is not a constant expression,
```
static T x = i;
```
may behave differently from
```
static T x;
// ...
x = i;
```
because initialization is performed only once, the first time control passes through the declaration. For example, given
```
static int j;
for (int i = 0; i < 10; ++i)
    {
    j = i;
    static int k = i;
    cout << j << ", " << k << "\n";
    }
```
the last line of output will be
```
9, 0
```
because k is only initialized the first time through.

JUSTIFICATION

Explicit initialization reduces code size and execution time. Declaring
```
T x (i);
```
invokes the constructor T::T(a) directly for x. In contrast,

```
T x;
// ...
x = i;
```

invokes the default constructor `T::T()` and later invokes the assignment `T::operator=(a)`.

Initialization can be written in several different ways that produce the same result. However, only

```
T x (i);
```

is guaranteed to apply a constructor directly to x. The other forms

```
T x = i;
T x = T(i);
T x = (T)i;
```

may create a temporary object of type T from i and copy it to x. However, E&S (1990) suggests that a good implementation will avoid creating unnecessary temporaries whenever possible. Therefore, programmers should choose whichever syntactic form of an initializer makes a declaration most readable, and trust compiler technology and/or future standardization to generate intelligent code. Using

```
T x = i;
```

to indicate an initial value, and using

```
T x (i);
```

to indicate a dimension is one example of favoring the most readable style.

ALTERNATIVES

To minimize any possibility of the creation and copying of temporaries, always use declarations of the form

```
T x (i);
```

instead of

```
T x = i;
T x = T(i);
T x = (T)i;
```

[LOCAL NOTES]

[LOCAL NOTES]

TOPIC: 1.11 const - concrete const vs. abstract const

GUIDELINE

A const object of a type that does not have a constructor or a destructor is said to be "concrete-const". (This definition implies that any const object of a Typesafe C type is always concrete-const. See Section 0.02.) A C++ translator may assume that the representation of a concrete-const object will not change, and thus may place that object in readonly memory (ROM). (Thus, the term "ROMable const" is equivalent to "concrete const".)

A const object of a class with a user-defined constructor or destructor is said to be "abstract-const". The representation of an abstract-const object may change during program execution, and so the translator is not free to place the object in ROM. The object's const-ness is defined by the class writer, as appropriate for abstract properties of the type.

The const member functions of an abstract-const object can alter the representation of the object by casting away the const-ness of *this. However, every const member function should preserve the client-visible value of the object.

EXAMPLE

A class token might have a member function hash that returns a hash value of a token. If computing the hash is expensive and some tokens never get hashed, then each object might defer computing its hash value until that value is requested. Once computed, the hash value could be stored inside the object to avoid recomputation until the token value changes.

Conceptually, hash should be applicable to const token objects because it doesn't alter the client-visible value of a token. However, hash alters the internal representation of a token by storing the computed hash value inside the object. But, if hash is a const member function, the type of this is const token * and assignment to the object's data members is prohibited. The hash value can be stored only by temporarily casting away the const-ness of *this inside hash, as follows:

48   Copyright © 1991, Thomas Plum and Dan Saks

```
    class token
        {
public:
    token(const char *s)
        {
        // ...
        hashed = 0;
        }
    unsigned long hash() const;
private:
    // ...
    int hashed;
    unsigned long hash_value;
    };

unsigned long token::hash() const
    {
    if (!hashed)
        {
        // compute hash value ...
        ((token *)this)->hash_value = /* ... */;
        ((token *)this)->hashed = 1;
        }
    return hash_value;
    }
```

GUIDELINE

If const objects of a class should be placed in ROM (whenever the compiler is capable of placing objects in ROM), then don't define a constructor or destructor for that class. Also, the initializer for each ROMable const object must be a value that can be determined at compile time.

Objects that are just-a-struct (Section 1.02) are often good candidates for placement in ROM. Thus, a type that is just-a-struct should not define a constructor or destructor.

Do not cast away the const-ness of a concrete-const object. In particular, do not cast away the const-ness of *this in a const member function unless the class is abstract-const. Every instance of casting away the const-ness of any class object (including *this) should be documented with an explanation that the cast is necessary and does not violate the abstract const-ness of the object.

JUSTIFICATION

Since a concrete-const may be placed in ROM, casting away the const-ness of a concrete-const object produces non-portable behavior depending on whether the object is actually in ROM. Providing at least one user-defined constructor or destructor insures that const objects of the type will be abstract-const and will not be placed in ROM. Casting away the const-ness of an abstract-const object is portable, and the resulting object behaves as if it were declared non-const.

E&S (1990) also notes that most machine architectures cannot make memory readonly during program execution. Thus, an object can be placed in ROM only if initial value is known at translation time. For example,

```
void foo(int i)
    {
    const int n = i;    // cannot go in ROM
    // ...
    }
```

E&S (1990) advises against casting away const in general because it violates a guarantee (made in a declaration) and makes a program harder to understand and debug. For example,

```
const char *greeting = "Hello";    // may be in ROM

void foo()
    {
    *(char *)greeting = 'Y';       // BAD - non-portable behavior
    }
```

ALTERNATIVES

Carroll (1990) suggests the following technique for minimizing the cast instances:

```
token *This = (token *)this;
This->hash_value = ...
This->hashed = 1;
```

Abstract-const is known in some circles as "meaning-const". Concrete-const is also known as "bitwise-const", or simply "bit-const".

[LOCAL NOTES]

[LOCAL NOTES]

TOPIC: 1.12 constfn - const member functions

STANDARD

If possible, declare member functions as const. This indicates to both the compiler and the human reader that the function does not modify its object, and can be invoked for both const objects and non-const objects. A function that modifies its object might still be a const function if the modification is not visible outside the class. (See Section 1.11 regarding "abstract const".)

If the function returns a pointer or reference to its object, or to a copy of its object, it may be necessary to overload on the const-ness of the object. For example,

```
class X
    {
    // ...
    X *clone() { return new X (*this); }          // clone a non-const X
            // OK to overload on const
    const X *clone() const { return new X (*this); } // clone a const X
    }
```

JUSTIFICATION

Both efficiency and readability are served by distinguishing "read-only" operations.

[LOCAL NOTES]

[LOCAL NOTES]

TOPIC: 1.13 friend - friend functions

GUIDELINE

In general, functions with access rights to a class should be members rather than friends of that class. Internal functions (used only by members and friends of the class) should always be members. Any functions to be inherited by a derived class, especially virtual functions, must be members.

Use a friend function when it is desirable for user-defined conversions to be applied to the function's first argument. This is typically appropriate for binary operator functions.

Use a friend function to implement a binary operator for class whose left operand is not an object of that class. For example,

```
friend ostream &X::operator<<(ostream &, const X &);
```

Use a friend function when (non-member) function call notation might preferred by customary usage to member function call notation. For example,

```
complex x, y;
//...
y = x.sqrt(); // member function call might look unnatural
y = sqrt(x);  // friend function call looks natural
```

This is not to say that member functions may not be used for mathematical types like complex, only that some projects may prefer non-member function calls for such types.

A function should not be a friend of more than one class.

To avoid ambiguities, if you declare that some other class's member function is a friend, use its qualified name. And when declaring a function to be a friend, do not define the function there. Define it elsewhere.

EXAMPLE

Friend functions are appropriate in classes of value-oriented objects like complex. Class complex can be defined with operator+ as a member function:

```
class complex
    {
    // ...
    complex(double);
    complex operator +(complex);              // inflexible
    };
```

or with `operator+` as a friend:

```
class complex
    {
    // ...
    complex(double);
    friend complex operator +(complex, complex); // flexible
    };
```

Using a friend function in preference to a member function increases the convenience of `operator+` by allowing user-defined conversions to be applied to the left operand as well as the right operand:

```
complex z1, z2;
double x;
// ...
z1 = z1 + z2;  // works with member or friend
z1 = z2 + x;   // works with member or friend
z1 = x + z2;   // works only with friend
```

x is converted to `complex` by applying `complex::complex(double)`.

JUSTIFICATION

Access to friend functions is not affected by the access specifiers `public`, `protected`, and `private`. The friends of class x are accessible in any scope in which x is declared. Thus friend functions should not be used for functions that are meant to be `protected` or `private`, and friend declarations should be placed among the `public` members.

Friend functions are not inherited, and cannot be virtual. Only members can be inherited.

The name of a member function is in the scope of its class, whereas the name of a friend function is global. Favoring member over friend functions reduces the size of the global name space and the potential for name conflicts.

Friend functions have no run-time performance advantages over non-virtual member functions. Calling a non-virtual, non-static member function with n arguments is as fast as calling a friend function with $n+1$ arguments. (The `this` pointer is implicitly passed as an argument to non-static member functions.)

Functions that are friends of more than one class increase coupling between classes and should be avoided.

ALTERNATIVES

Declaring a function as a friend of two classes may provide a faster
and simpler interface between the classes by bypassing (or even eliminating) restrictive access functions provided by the classes for general
users. E&S (1990) suggest this example:

```
class Vector;

class Matrix
    {
    friend Vector operator+(const Matrix &, const Vector &);
    // ...
    };

class Vector
    {
    friend Vector operator+(const Matrix &, const Vector &);
    // ...
    };
```

Mutual friendship should be used sparingly.

[LOCAL NOTES]

[LOCAL NOTES]

TOPIC: 1.14 static - static data members

GUIDELINE

Use static data members instead of global objects to store data that must be shared by all objects of a class.

EXAMPLE

A class with overloaded new and delete that maintains its own list of available storage should store the bookkeeping for that list in static data members. Furthermore, these static members should be private, because the storage management technique should not be known outside the class.

JUSTIFICATION

Static data members are part of a class and obey the same access rules as non-static members (except that static data members can be initialized at file scope). Therefore, using static data members instead of global objects improves readability and maintainability by restricting the access to shared data. Using static data members also reduces the possibility of global naming conflicts (Section 1.04).

ALTERNATIVES

If your project has decided that minimizing re-compilations is the major priority, the guideline on static members is quite different. (See Section 6.11.)

[LOCAL NOTES]

[LOCAL NOTES]

TOPIC: 1.15 paramtypes - parameterized types

GUIDELINE

Use templates to define a family of classes as a single "generic" class when the differences in structure and implementation among the family members can be characterized by a small set of type parameters.

General container classes such as vector and stack should be implemented as templates. For example, the definition

```
template <class T> class vector
    {
    T *vec;
    size_t size;
public:
    vector(size_t);
    T &operator [](size_t);
    // ...
    };
```

enables the declaration of vectors for a wide range of element types, such as

```
vector<double> v1 (100);
vector<int> v2 (200);
```

Synthesized mathematical types, such as complex and rational, can also be implemented as templates. For example,

```
rational<long> r1;
rational<short> r2;
```

allows the client application to control the size and precision of rational numbers.

Use parameterized types to implement a "generic" function, like abs, max, or sort, that applies the same algorithm to a variety of types. For example,

```
template <class T> T abs(T a)
    {
    return (a < 0) ? -a : a;
    }
```

Do not use polymorphism (derived classes with virtual functions) to implement parameterized types. That is, do not define containers of polymorphic objects derived from a common object type like Object or common. Also, do not implement generic containers as containers of void *. Programs that must be supported on C++ implementations without templates should simulate parameterized types using a mechanism that preserves static typing, or avoid parameterized types altogether (Section 7.06).

Copyright © 1991, Thomas Plum and Dan Saks

EXAMPLE

Note there is a subtle, but important, difference between a general-purpose container of a common, application-independent abstract base class and a container of an application-specific base class. For example, it is possible to implement both a linked-list of student and a linked-list of classroom by implementing a linked-list of Object, and deriving both student and classroom from Object. This guideline discourages the approach, suggesting that templates are the more appropriate implementation technique:

```
template <class T> class list
    {
    // ...
    };


// ...
list<student> roster;
list<classroom> available[HOURS];
```

This guideline does not discourage implementing single-purpose containers of abstract base class objects. For example, a user interface package may support a variety of window types, all derived from a base class window. An application using this package may need lists of windows:

```
class Window
    {
    virtual void draw();
    virtual void resize();
    // ...
    };

class TextWindow : public Window { ... };
class GraphicalWindow : public Window { ... };

class WindowList
    {
public:
    WindowList();
    // ...
private:
    struct node
        {
        node *next;
        Window *w;
        };
    node *first;
    };
```

This technique is valid. However, using an existing template class for lists might save some effort:

```
typedef List<Window> WindowList;
```

JUSTIFICATION

Template classes and functions provide an efficient, type-safe way to define homogeneous container classes for a wide range of component types. A "homogeneous" container can only hold objects of a single type. In the vast majority of applications, this is exactly what is required. Template containers can guarantee homogeneity at compile-time without run-time overhead.

Containers with polymorphic objects are "heterogeneous". They allow different types of objects to be inadvertently mixed in a single container. They can only enforce homogeneity via run-time checking.

Containers of void * are containers of typeless objects. They are unsafe and should be avoided.

Template functions, such as abs and max, are as flexible as macros. If inline'd, template functions can be just as efficient as macros, but without the restrictions on argument side-effects required by "unprotected" macros.

ALTERNATIVES

In the rare event that a heterogeneous container is required, implement it as a container of polymorphic objects.

[LOCAL NOTES]

[LOCAL NOTES]

TOPIC: 1.16 names - choosing variable names

GUIDELINE

Names should be chosen to be meaningful; their meaning should be *exact* and should be preserved throughout the program.

For example, variables which count something should be initialized to the count which is valid at that point; i.e., if the count is initially zero, the variable should be initialized to 0, not to -1 or some other number.

This means that each variable has an *invariant* (i.e. unchanging) meaning — a property that is true throughout the program. The readability of the code is enhanced by *minimizing the "domains of exceptions"*, which are the regions of the program in which the invariant property fails. For example, in this short loop, the variable nc has the invariant property of being equal to the number of characters read so far. The only exception to the property is during the time between reading a character and incrementing the counter:

```
short nc;    // number of characters

nc = 0;
while (getchar() != EOF)
     ++nc;
```

Abbreviations for meaningful names should be chosen by a uniform scheme. For example, use the leading consonant of each word in a name.

Abbreviations should not form letter combinations that suggest unintended meanings; the name inch is a misleading abbreviation for "input character". Similarly, names should not create misleading phonemes; the name metach (abbreviation for "meta-character") forms the phonemes "me-tach" in English, obscuring the meaning.

Names should not be re-defined in inner blocks.

A special case of meaningful names is the use of standard short names like c for characters, i, j, k for indexes, n for counters, p or q for pointers, s for strings, and x, y, z for (floating-point) mathematical variables.

In separate functions, variables with identical meanings can have the same name. But when the meanings are only similar or coincidental, use different names.

Names over four characters in length should differ by at least two characters:

```
systst, sysstst // bad - easily confused
```

The following abbreviations can be used within comments for greater precision:

```
nul                means the char value '\0'
a[i:j]             means the subarray a[i] through a[j]
a[*]               means the entire array a (for emphasis)
p[*]               means the entire array accessed through p
a[*] => sorted     means that a[*] is now sorted
```

Include "one-too-far" values in the ranges for variables, if they are needed for loop terminations or other testing purposes.

Document the defining properties of declared names in a comment on the declaration. To encourage use of such comments, and to create the potential for future automation of property-checking, use a concise convention such as "space, colon, space, property name". Example:

```
int hand;   // which hand : {1:2}
```

Choose project-wide consistent names for the important properties of data, and use these names in the documenting comments. Examples:

```
{lo:hi}         means the range from lo to hi .

{>lo:<hi}       means the range of values greater than lo and less
                than hi.
{lo, b:c, hi}   means the range of values lo, b through c, and hi.

bits(n)         used for bitwise operations on n bits.

bool            tested for either false (zero) or true (non-zero).

string          contains a null-terminator (for array of chars, or
                array of chars designated by a pointer).
dollars         represents currency in dollars; i.e. the value 12.34
                means 12 dollars and 34 cents.
pennies         represents currency in pennies; i.e. the value 12.34
                means 12 and 34/100 cents.
```

The dollars and pennies properties illustrate the use of "property comments" for units of measure; other instances might be meters, grams, seconds, etc. Always indicate units of measure whenever appropriate.

Ensure that the defining properties remain invariant (unchanging) as much as possible throughout the computation, and document any exceptions.

Do not use the same variable for different purposes.

An array is *complete* if none of its elements are in an undefined (uninitialized or "garbage") state. A program is easier to write correctly and to understand if all arrays are made complete before the array is used.

If an array's defining property can be true even if some elements are in an undefined state, indicate the property on the array's declaration. For example,

```
char message[10];     // : string
```

Use executable assertions whenever they are simpler than the code being protected, and when the time to execute the assertions is not much greater than the time required to execute the code.

A class object (just-a-struct or a class) is *well-defined* if the values of all its members have whatever defining properties were specified in comments. This carries out the rule of "minimizing the domains of exceptions". Thus, for example, if a member is specified to have a range of values like ⟨0:9⟩, that member must have a value between 0 and 9 in order for the object to be considered well-defined. For class objects, it is the responsibility of the constructor to ensure that the initial value is well-defined.

If a just-a-struct is not well-defined when initialized to zero, document this fact in a comment. (The program will in general be simpler if the members are defined such that the zero-initialized structure is well-defined.)

JUSTIFICATION

Readability of the code is greatly enhanced by the reader's ability to construct natural assertions about the meaning of names anywhere they appear in the code, and about the specific properties of the data.

[LOCAL NOTES]

[LOCAL NOTES]

TOPIC: 1.17 stdtypes - standard defined-types

STANDARD

Programs should use a project-wide standard set of data-type names.

The set of standard types presented here are a mixture of standard C++ types (sometimes with usage restrictions) and defined-types defined by the header portdefs.h. (All the headers described in these guidelines are described in detail in Section 4.23.)

There are three purposes for this usage of types: portability to the widest range of machines and compilers, semantic clarity regarding the usage of the data, and brevity.

```
char      - an 8+ bit item used only for characters and memory bytes

schar     - an 8+ bit signed integer (signed char)
short     - a 16+ bit signed integer (short int)
long      - a 32+ bit signed integer (long int)

uchar     - an 8+ bit unsigned integer (unsigned char)
ushort    - a 16+ bit unsigned integer (unsigned short)
ulong     - a 32+ bit unsigned integer (unsigned long)

float     - single precision floating point number
double    - double precision floating point number
ldouble   - long double precision floating point number (long double)

bool      - int (or smaller), tested only for zero or non-zero
metachar  - some integer, to hold a character or an end-of-file flag
textchar  - char or wchar_t, to hold a character (narrow or wide)
int       - for function parameters, returned values and registers
uint      - unsigned int (parameters, returned values and registers)

size_t    - an unsigned integer, for holding the size of an object
```

Avoid careless dependence on the int size of the computer. This is especially important on machines where int and long are the same size; careless code will not port correctly down to smaller machines.

There are, however, three uses of the int (or uint) type which are appropriate for portable programs. First of all, a function's returned value may be written as int. (Many existing library functions are defined to have int returned values.) The second portable usage of int is for function parameters, again for consistency with standard libraries. The third usage of int is for register integer variables. In all these usages, programs should assume that int contains at least 16 bits and perhaps more.

Most of these defined-types are created at the choice of the project, but one of them is defined in several Standard headers: `size_t` is the proper type for holding the `sizeof` any object. It is the proper type for the storage size passed to allocation functions such as `calloc`.

For maximum portability, programs should not make assumptions about the size of pointer-to-function.

Programs must use the semantically correct data-type name, even where several similar names map onto the same raw C language type.

Bitwise operations should be performed upon unsigned data, for maximum portability.

[LOCAL NOTES]

TOPIC: 1.18 constants - maintainability of constants

STANDARD

Any constant which might change during revision or modification should be "manifest" ("clearly apparent to the sight or understanding; obvious"). Specifically, it should be given an upper-case name.

If it is only used in one file, it should be defined at the head of that file; if used in multiple files, it should be defined in a header.

Standard manifest constants should be used where appropriate. Examples from <stdio.h>:

```
BUFSIZ      the size of a standard file buffer
NULL        zero, as a pointer value
EOF         the end-of-file return value from getchar
SEEK_SET    seek relative to file start
SEEK_CUR    seek relative to current position
SEEK_END    seek relative to file end
```

Always terminate successful execution of the main function with

```
return 0;
```

Terminate successful execution in other functions with

```
exit(0);
```

In strictly portable programs, unsuccessful execution should be terminated using the manifest constant EXIT_FAILURE from <stdlib.h>:

```
exit(EXIT_FAILURE);
```

If there are limitations on the modifiability of a defined constant, indicate the limitations with a comment:

```
#define EOF (-1)  /* DO NOT MODIFY: ctype.h expects -1 */
```

If one definition affects another, embody the relationship in the definition; do not give two independent definitions.

If a value is given for a defined name, do not defeat its modifiability by assuming its value in expressions.

When defining manifest constants for array bounds and subscript limits, use the number of elements rather than the index of the last element (in zero-origin C, these differ by one).

Write programs as if enumeration variables could receive no values other than the associated enumeration constants.

Copyright © 1991, Thomas Plum and Dan Saks

JUSTIFICATION

Constants that are hard-coded (otherwise known as "magic numbers" because they mysteriously appear with no explanation) are hard to locate when modifying the program. Furthermore, instances of "constant minus one" or "constant plus one" are even more elusive to the maintenance programmer.

EXAMPLE

```
if (index < 100)        // bad - no explanation, hard to modify

const int SIZE = 100;   // good (preferred in C++) - or ...
enum {SIZE=100};        // also good (especially inside classes) - or ...
#define SIZE 100         // ok (but see Section 4.05)
    ...
if (index < SIZE)       // good
```

[LOCAL NOTES]

TOPIC: 1.19 wordlen - word and byte size

STANDARD

C programs should assume the following sizes for data:

```
char    8 bits (or more)

short   16 bits (or more)

long    32 bits (or more)
```

The following rule is necessary for porting to the widest variety of target machines and compilers: A program should never rely on data size (or casts) to truncate expressions to a specific number of bits. Use masks (bit-and) to produce a specific number of bits.

If, alternatively, the project has determined that all future targets will be 8-16-32 environments, such restrictions are not necessary. But then this limitation should be clearly stated in project specifications or atop source files, headers, etc.

Bitwise constants can be made more portable by relying on the "bit-not" operator to set high-order one-bits. For example, to turn off the low-order bit of a variable b:

```
b &= ~1;        /* good */

b &= 0177776;   /* bad - turns off high bits */
                /*       on 32-bit machine   */
```

JUSTIFICATION

The object of this standard is portability. There are compilers with char's of 8, 9, or 10 bits, with short's of 16, 18, 20, and 36 bits, and with long's of 32, 36, and 40 bits. And even within the eight-bit world, bitwise constants are subject to the uncertainty of the int size.

[LOCAL NOTES]

[LOCAL NOTES]

TOPIC: 1.20 byteorder - byte ordering

STANDARD

Portability demands that programs not depend upon the order of bytes within an integral or floating number. For example, on some machines, the low-order byte of a short integer is stored in memory before the high-order byte; but on other machines, the high-order byte is stored first.

In portable code, question each appearance of a pointer cast:

```
char *p;
short n;

p = (char *)&n; // bad - non-portable, machine-dependent byte
```

Binary data written on one machine will be portable to another machine only if byte-ordering dependencies are eliminated. A canonical ordering for binary data must be chosen. Before writing binary data, it should be converted to this canonical order; after reading canonical binary data, it should be converted back. The same considerations apply to floating data.

JUSTIFICATION

It is possible to write C programs which will give identical results on machines with different byte-orders, but one must follow the rules given above.

[LOCAL NOTES]

[LOCAL NOTES]

TOPIC: 1.21 charconsts - character constants

STANDARD

Portability requires that character constants not contain more than one character. The differences in machine byte-order may cause multi-character constants to differ either in numeric value or in character sequence.

EXAMPLE

```
short crlf = '\r\n';    // bad - uses char constant
```

If the characters are simply being used as a string value, use a proper C string:

```
char crlf[] = "\r\n";   // good - uses string constant
```

Often, multi-character constants are introduced in order to make a single integer value from two or more char's for example to switch on the value. In such cases, there is a portable means to achieve the same efficiency:

```
#define CHAR2(a, b)  (((a) << CHAR_BIT) + (b))
...
switch (CHAR2(c1, c2))
    {
case CHAR2('e', 'd'):
    /* ... */
```

JUSTIFICATION

The multi-character constants are intrinsically non-portable.

[LOCAL NOTES]

[LOCAL NOTES]

TOPIC: 1.22 ptrtypes - pointer types

STANDARD

Pointers which will point to several different types of object may be declared as void * generic pointers.

However, in C++, each use of a void * represents a failure to achieve type safety, and needs to be questioned. If the pointer is a parameter, it may be possible to provide a set of overloaded functions, each of which accepts a specific pointer type. It may be possible to eliminate the void * by using a template class or function. And if the pointed-to types are conceptually related, then the underlying design may properly be object-oriented and should be implemented with inheritance.

Pointers-to-functions should be given typedef'ed types, to improve the conceptual clarity:

```
/* an INT_F_INT is a pointer to function of int arg returning int */
typedef int (*INT_F_INT)(int);

INT_F_INT pfa;   /* a pointer whose type is INT_F_INT */
```

In some environments, pointers-to-data and pointers-to-function have different sizes and representations. The void * generic pointers should contain only addresses of data, and not of functions. In particular, the symbol NULL should not be used with pointers-to-functions. A simple integer constant zero will suffice for the occasional "null pointer-to-function", as in

```
int func(
    INT_F_INT pfa)  /* one pointer argument */
    (
    if (pfa == 0)
        /* handle the null-pointer case  ... */
    /* ... */
```

[LOCAL NOTES]

[LOCAL NOTES]

TOPIC: 1.23 ptrconv - pointer conversions

STANDARD

Programs should contain no pointer conversions, except for the following safe ones:

0 may be assigned to any pointer-to-data.

Pointers to an object of a given size may be converted to a pointer-to-character or a generic pointer and back again, without change. For example, a pointer-to-long may be assigned to a pointer-to-character variable which is later assigned back to a pointer-to-long. Any use of the intermediate pointer, other than equality-tests or assigning it back to the original type, gives machine-dependent code.

Integers (properly cast) may be assigned to pointers, or pointers (properly cast) to integers, but *only* in non-portable hardware-dependent functions, such as device drivers.

JUSTIFICATION

Other conversions will be compiler-dependent or machine-dependent, or both.

EXAMPLE

```
short *pi;
char *pc;

pi = 0;      // ok to assign 0

pc = pi;     // ok to assign to char pointer
pi = pc;     // and then assign back to larger-type

// Non-portable (e.g., device driver) examples ...
ioport = (short *)0xA220;       // hardware-dependent I/O port address
offset = (int)buf_addr & 0x1FF; // hardware-dependent bit manipulation
```

[LOCAL NOTES]

[LOCAL NOTES]

TOPIC: 1.24 alloc - allocation integrity

STANDARD

A function in which the address of an automatic variable is assigned to a non-automatic pointer must contain a comment to that effect. In any function with such a comment, each return from the function is an event requiring verification that no dangling pointers are left.

When a pointer p is passed to the free function or the delete operator, the programmer must determine how many pointers are pointing into the freed storage. (This number is known as the "reference count" of the storage.) Steps must be taken (such as assigning 0 to such pointers) to ensure that none of these pointers are subsequently used to access the freed storage.

For every instance in which a program allocates storage, there should be an easily identifiable instance in which that storage is later freed. This is one reason why C++ has destructors. If the allocation is in the constructor, the deallocation would ordinarily be placed in the destructor.

For every instance of fopen, there should be an easily identifiable instance of fclose (and perhaps an ferror test too — see Section 5.05). Again, constructors and destructors are logical places for such "open" and "close" operations.

[LOCAL NOTES]

[LOCAL NOTES]

TOPIC: 1.25 structs - structures

STANDARD

In portable programming, do not hard-code the numeric values of structure offsets. The values may be different in each environment. Refer to members by their symbolic member names only. If the numeric offset of a structure member (in just-a-struct) is needed, use the macro offsetof from <stddef.h>. (See Section 7.02.)

In portable code, do not depend upon the allocation order of bit-fields within a word. Do not depend upon having more than 16 bits per word.

[LOCAL NOTES]

[LOCAL NOTES]

TOPIC: 1.26 strings - string literals

STANDARD

String literals should not be modified. To achieve a modifiable string, use a named array of characters.

In other words, if `mktemp` is a function that modifies its string argument, do not write

```
mktemp("/tmp/edXXXXXX");
```

Instead, use a named array:

```
static char fname[] = "/tmp/edXXXXXX";

mktemp(fname);
```

[LOCAL NOTES]

Copyright © 1991, Thomas Plum and Dan Saks

[LOCAL NOTES]

TOPIC: 2.01 temp - dynamics of temporaries

GUIDELINE

Avoid creating unnecessary temporaries. For example, if a vector class
provides both `operator+` and `operator+=`, and assuming

```
v1 = v1 + v2;
```
and
```
v1 += v2;
```

yield the same result, then use the latter form. It is likely to create
fewer temporaries (see Section 2.01).

Do not create dangling pointers or dangling references to temporaries.
Do not depend upon the exact timing of the destruction of temporaries. It is guaranteed, however, that a temporary created as an
argument to a reference parameter will endure until the function
returns.

JUSTIFICATION

The exact point of destruction for temporaries is version-dependent.
Pointers to the internal representation of temporary objects can easily
become dangling pointers. E&S (1990) provides the following example:

```
class String
    {
private:
    char *s;
public:
    operator char*() { return s; }
    friend String operator+(const String &, const String &)
    // ...
    };

void foo(const char *s)
    {
    // ...
    }
```

```
String s1("foo"), s2("bar");
```
The call
```
foo(s1 + s2);
```
may be implemented as

```
construct s1 + s2 in temp1
put (char *)temp1 into temp2
destroy temp1
foo(temp2)
```

As another example, suppose class Mutex provides resource locking and unlocking to implement mutual exclusion:

```
Mutex m;
// ...
m.lock();
// critical section for exclusive access to a resource
m.unlock();
```

If the critical section creates a temporary object with access to the locked resource, the temporary should be destroyed before the resource is unlocked, but there's no guarantee that it will be. If the temporary is destroyed after the resource is unlocked, the destructor may modify the resource, even though another process may have entered the critical section. This violates the mutual exclusion, and may corrupt the resource.

Recent discussion in the ANSI C++ standards committee indicate that the eventual standard will specify short lifetimes for temporaries. However, temporaries created while evaluating the arguments to a function call will probably endure until after the function returns.

[LOCAL NOTES]

TOPIC: 2.02 overload – managing overloading

GUIDELINE

There is a temptation to overload operators just because they are available. The classic "master file update" design problem *can* be implemented in C++, with immense effort, as

```
newMasterFile = oldMasterFile + updateFile;      // BAD - good grief!
```

Resist the temptation. Be sure there is a real justification for the overloading.

One acceptable reason is "common practice", such as the `abs` function.

JUSTIFICATION

Numerous projects report that operator overloading was over-used, in their initial fascination with the technique, and that it detracted from system clarity.

GUIDELINE

As much as possible, overloaded operators should preserve the intuitive properties of the operator being overloaded.

For example, the arithmetic conversion rules of C++ (and C) go to some trouble to allow programmers to think about *values* rather than specific data types:

```
x = y + 5;
```

has a fairly intuitive meaning regardless of the exact types of x and y. Do not violate this intuition by providing different semantics for different arithmetic types. (The typical implementation of complex arithmetic is a good example in this regard.)

These are the intuitive properties of the overloadable operators; operand descriptions such as `"array"` mean that the operand has properties "like an array".

```
x(y)      invokes a "function"
x[y]      x is "array"; produces a reference
x->y      x is "pointer"; produces a reference
!x        produces "Boolean"; self-inverse (x and !!x are same value)
~x        produces "bits"; self-inverse (x and ~~x are same value)
++x       x is "lvalue"; adds 1 before evaluation; identical to x+=1
x++       x is "lvalue"; adds 1 after evaluation
+x        same value as x
-x        negation of x; self-inverse [ x and -(-x) are same value ]
&x        x is "lvalue"; address of x
*x        x is "pointer"; produces a reference
x*y       commutative; associative; x*1 equals 1*x equals x
x/y       anti-commutative [ (x/y) * (y/x) equals 1 ]; inverse of *
x%y       -
x+y       commutative; associative; x+0 equals 0+x equals x
x-y       anti-commutative [ (x-y) + (y-x) equals 0 ]; inverse of +
x<<y      -
x>>y      -
x<y       produces "Boolean"; same as  !(x >= y)
x<=y      produces "Boolean"; same as  !(x > y)
x>y       produces "Boolean"; same as  !(x <= y)
x>=y      produces "Boolean"; same as  !(x < y)
x==y      produces "Boolean"; same as  !(x != y)
x!=y      produces "Boolean"; same as  !(x == y)
x&y       produces "bits"; commutative; associative
x^y       produces "bits"; commutative; associative
x|y       produces "bits"; commutative; associative
x&&y      produces "Boolean"; sequenced; short-circuit (skip y if x FALSE)
x||y      produces "Boolean"; sequenced; short-circuit (skip y if x TRUE)
x op= y   same as  x = (x op y) except x eval'ed once only; x is "lvalue"
x,y       produces y; sequenced
```

Because any form of overloading destroys the "sequenced" property of
&&, ||, and comma, these operators should seldom (if ever) be over-
loaded.

The use of overloaded () for iterators is discouraged, in favor of
explicitly named next member functions.

Besides the analysis of operand properties given above, consideration
also needs to be given to precedence. For example, overloading ^
(exclusive-or) to serve as exponentiation for floating-point or complex
operands would violate conventional expectations for the binding of
a * b ^ c.

It is recognized that "intuitive" is subjective to some extent, and that a
popular class library may establish a new "intuitive" meaning. For
example, the use of << and >> in the streams library may now be more
widespread than the use of the actual left-shift and right-shift operators. Similarly, the typical use of + for string catenation is associative
but not commutative; still, it is the most intuitive choice.

JUSTIFICATION

Readability, reliability, and maintainability all require that the meaning of the code be intuitively graspable.

GUIDELINE

If assignment is not a desirable operation for a class, declare but do not define, a private assignment operator. For example, assignment is usually inappropriate for file or stream objects. Declare

```
class file
    {
private:
    file &operator =(const file &);
    // ...
    };
```

but do not implement the function.

JUSTIFICATION

If `operator=` is not declared for a class, the compiler creates a default version. Explicitly declaring `X::operator=` prevents the compiler from creating the default version. If `X::operator=` is not implemented, any attempt to use it will be caught as a link error.

GUIDELINE

Declare a binary operator `op` for a class x as a friend function, using

```
friend X operator op(const X &, const X &);
```

Declare an assignment operator `op=` for a class x as a member, using

```
X &operator op=(const X &);
```

JUSTIFICATION

Binary operators like + should be implemented as friends to allow user-defined conversions to be applied to both operands (Section 1.13). Assignment operators like += should be implemented as class members because the left operand should be an object of the class.

GUIDELINE

The implementation of overloaded binary operators for a class depends on the storage management for that class. A class is fixed-sized if copying into an object of that class (using = or op=) cannot change the amount of free store used to represent that object. A class that is not fixed-sized is variable-sized.

When overloading a binary operator op for a class x for which assignment is defined, implement op= first. If x is fixed-size and the implementation of op= is non-trivial, then implement op in terms of op=. If op= is trivial, implement op directly in terms of the data members of x.

EXAMPLE

Class rational is a fixed-size class representing signed rational numbers (fractions). Operator += is sufficiently complicated to warrant implementing + in terms of +=:

```
class rational
    {
public:
    rational &operator+=(const rational &r);
    friend rational operator+
        (const rational &r1, const rational &r2);
    // ...
private:
    long num, denom;            // numerator and denominator
    };

rational &rational::operator+=(const rational &r)
    {
    num = num * r.denom + r.num * denom;
    denom = denom * r.denom;
    long d = gcd(num, denom);  // greatest common divisor
    num /= d;
    denom /= d;
    return *this;
    }

rational rational::operator+
    (const rational &r1, const rational &r2)
    {
    rational r = r1
    return r += r2;
    }
```

Class complex implements complex numbers in rectangular coordinate form. Operator + is so simple, it need not be implemented in terms of +=:

```
class complex
    {
public:
    complex(double, double);
    // ...
private:
    double re, im;              // real and imaginary
    };

complex &complex::operator+=(const complex &z)
    {
    re += z.re;
    im += z.im;
    return *this;
    }


friend complex complex::operator+
    (const complex &z1, const complex &z2);
    {
    return complex(z1.re + z2.re, z1.im + z.im);
    }
```

GUIDELINE

If class x is variable-sized and the amount of free store used by the
result of binary operator op is the same as the amount used by one of
the operands, then implement op in terms of op=. For example, opera-
tor+ for a vector can be defined to add two vector of unequal length
by extending the shorter vector with zeroes. The result will have the
same length as the longer argument. In this case, implement + in
terms of += as follows

```
friend Vector Vector::operator+
    (const Vector &v1, const Vector &v2)
    {
    Vector v = (v1.size() > v2.size()) ? v1 : v2;
    return v += (v1.size() > v2.size()) ? v2 : v1;
    }
```

If class x is variable-sized and the amount of free store used by the
result of binary operator op is different from the amount used by
either operand, then do not implement op in terms of op=. If the
implementation of both op and op= is sufficiently complex, implement
the common logic in a private member function of x (possibly a constructor).

EXAMPLE

String concatenation constructs a new string whose size is large enough
to hold both operands. That construction can be performed by a
private concatenation constructor invoked by both operator+ and

operator+=:

```
class String
    {
    String(const String &, const String &);
        // construct a string by concatenation
public:
    String operator+(const String &s1, const String &s2)
        {
        return String(s1, s2);
        }
    String &operator+=(const String &s)
        {
        return *this = String(*this, s);
        }
    };
```

JUSTIFICATION

A good implementation of op= is usually more efficient than the implementation of the corresponding op. The implementation of op typically creates and copies temporary objects. op= rarely requires temporaries. For example, x += y adds the value of y into the existing copy of x. On the other hand, x + y can modify neither x nor y, so it creates a temporary for the result.

In the case of the vector class where operator+ can add vectors of unequal size, careful ordering of the operations avoids unnecessary copying. If v1 is shorter than v2, v1 += v2 computes the result in a newly constructed vector the size of v2. The old contents of v1 are discarded when the new vector is assigned to v1. If v1 is as long or longer than v2, the result is computed directly in v1 and no constructors or destructors are called. operator+ always constructs a new vector to hold the result. If operator+ were implemented as simply

```
friend Vector Vector::operator+
    (const Vector &v1, const Vector &v2)
    {
    Vector v = v1;
    return v += v2;
    }
```

then whenever v1 is shorter than v2, the call to operator+= will allocate storage for a larger vector, and discard the initial storage. Initializing v to the longer vector avoids unnecessary allocation, deallocation and copying.

With string concatenation, expressing operator+ in terms of operator+=, or vice versa, requires copying to and from extra temporaries. For example, consider

Copyright © 1991, Thomas Plum and Dan Saks   95

```
String String::operator+(const String &s1, const String &s2)
    {
    String s = s1;
    return s += s2;
    }
```

This implementation initializes `s` with the value of `s1`. However, `s +=`
`s2` constructs a new, longer string to hold the result and discards the
initial storage for `s`. A concatenation constructor avoids this unnecessary initialization.

ALTERNATIVES

If `sizeof(X)` is small enough, the operands of `op` and `op=` can be passed
by value rather than by reference. The declarations for the operators
look like

```
friend X operator op(X, X);
```
and
```
X &operator op=(X);
```

GUIDELINE

If "address-of" (`&`) is overloaded in a base class, it should be overloaded in each derived class.

JUSTIFICATION

The returned type should point to the specific type. It is counter-
intuitive for "address-of" to point to a type different from the
operand.

REFERENCES

Cargill 1990 "Does Operator Overloading Help Systems Programmers?"

[LOCAL NOTES]

[LOCAL NOTES]

TOPIC: 2.03 newdel - overloading new and delete

GUIDELINE

In general, individual components of a large program should not redefine the global operators new and delete (denoted ::new and ::delete, respectively).

If, for purposes of debugging or profiling, ::new and ::delete are redefined, the redefinitions should be part of the test driver software or a test support library, and not part of the tested components. For example, ::new and ::delete can be augmented to detect errors such as freeing storage that's already free or freeing storage that's not in the free store.

After system-wide profiling, ::new and ::delete may be redefined to improve a program's execution speed or reduce its memory consumption. Alternative memory management algorithms may out-perform the general storage allocator supplied by the C++ translator.

The operators new and delete defined for a class X are denoted X::new and X::delete, respectively. Define X::new and X::delete when:

1.   a typical application allocates and frees many objects of type X, and X::new and X::delete can be made significantly faster than ::new and ::delete;

2.   allocating and freeing objects of type X causes excessive fragmentation in the free store, and X::new and X::delete can reduce that fragmentation significantly, or ::new and X::new may be overloaded with additional arguments, and invoked using the *placement syntax*.

However, the first argument of any definition of new should be of type size_t. For example, invoke

```
void *X::operator new(size_t, void *);
```
with a call

```
p = new(buf) X;
```
The most commonly accepted overloading is to add a second argument that specifies the region of memory from which the object should be allocated. This is useful for managing different types of memory, such as the near and far heaps characteristic of MS-DOS systems.

A class with a constructor that defines X::new with more than one argument should also define X::new with just one argument (of type size_t). An implementation may place a call to operator new (with one argument)

in the body of a constructor. Any overloading of x::new obscures the
global operator new. If class doesn't define x::new with a single argument, the compiler won't be able to find any new to satisfy the constructor.

Do not assign to this in a constructor or destructor.

JUSTIFICATION

Earlier C++ translators provided assignment to this as a means of controlling storage allocation. Assignment to this proved to be awkward
and error-prone, and has been superceded by overloading of new and
delete.

E&S (1990) suggest that redefining ::new and ::delete is useful for
debugging, but not recommended for programming in general. If different components of a large program overload ::new and ::delete differently, the components may not work together when integrated.

[LOCAL NOTES]

TOPIC: 2.04 casts - keep casts significant

STANDARD

Each occurrence of a cast should alert the reader to some special need to override the type system of C or C++. Do not adopt any style rule which insert casts routinely for insignificant reasons.

EXAMPLE

Many C lint processors are deficient in not distinguishing between important return values and incidental return values. They warn every time a return value is ignored, which leads to programming styles like this:

```
(void)strcpy(a, b);
```

JUSTIFICATION

Each cast needs to be examined, to determine whether it masks some portability problem. Requiring wholesale casts diminishes their alerting value.

[LOCAL NOTES]

[LOCAL NOTES]

TOPIC: 2.05 cast - casting objects

GUIDELINE

In general, do not cast a pointer or reference to one object type into a pointer or reference to another object type. However, the following conversion patterns are reasonably safe and portable:

1   A pointer to an object type may be converted to a void * and then cast back to the original pointer type.

2.   If class D is derived from class B, and B is not a virtual base class, and there is an unambiguous conversion from D to B, then a B* may be cast to a D*, or a B& may be cast to a D&. The referenced base class object must be a sub-object of the resulting derived class object. The resulting D* (D&) may be converted back to a B* (B&) without a cast.

Do not convert a pointer to a function type into a pointer to an object type or void *, or vice versa. Do not cast away the const-ness of an object except in the implementation of an abstract-const class (Section 1.11).

JUSTIFICATION

E&S (1990) describe various other explicit conversions that are allowed in certain circumstances. For example, a pointer of type T1* can be converted to a T2* and back if sizeof(T1) >= sizeof(T2). Clearly, code that relies on the relative sizes of T1 and T2 can easily be broken if either type is modified.

As another example, a pointer to a function can be converted to a void * if void * has sufficient bits. Given the variations in data object sizes among different architectures, code that relies on these relative sizes of pointer types will not be portable.

Thoughtful use of inheritance and virtual functions eliminates most uses for casts.

EXAMPLE

Casting pointers to objects with virtual functions can produce very subtle bugs. The cast converts the data members and non-virtual functions to a different type, but the virtual functions remain unchanged. The following illustrates the consequences:

```
#include <stdio.h>

class B
    {
public:
    virtual void foo() { printf("I'm a B\n"); }
    };

class D1 : public B
    {
    char *p;
public:
    D1(char *pp) : p(pp) { }
    void foo() { printf("I'm a D1, and my value is %s\n", p); }
    void bar() { printf("I'm a D1, and my value is %s\n", p); }
    };

class D2 : public B
    {
    int i;
public:
    D2(int ii) : i(ii) { }
    void foo() { printf("I'm a D2, and my value is %d\n", i); }
    void bar() { printf("I'm a D2, and my value is %d\n", i); }
    };

int main()
    {
    D1 d1("hello");
    d1.foo();               // OK - calls D1::foo()
    d1.bar();               // OK - calls D1::bar()
    B *pb = &d1;            // OK - uses standard conversion
    pb->foo();              // OK - calls D1::foo()
    D2 *pd2 = (D2 *)&d1;   // BAD - pd2 becomes schizophrenic
    pd2->foo();             // ??? - calls D1::foo()
    pd2->bar();             // ??? - calls D2::bar()
    return 0;
    }
```

pd2 points to an object that sometimes behaves like a D2, and at other times behaves like a D1. The output of the program looks like:

```
I'm a D1, and my value is hello
I'm a D1, and my value is hello
I'm a D1, and my value is hello
I'm a D1, and my value is hello
I'm a D2, and my value is 96
```

[LOCAL NOTES]

TOPIC: 2.06 evalorder - allowable dependencies on evaluation order

STANDARD

Programs should not depend upon the order of evaluation of expressions, except as guaranteed for the following operators:

```
1.  a, b        comma operator (not the comma between args)
2.  a && b      logical and
3.  a || b      logical or
4.  a ? b : c   conditional
```

All of these guarantee that expression a will be computed before expression b (or c). In case 4, exactly one of the two expressions b and c will be evaluated.

Furthermore, when a function-call takes place, all the arguments are fully evaluated before control transfers to the function. Thus, in

```
5.  a(b)        function-call
```

the operand b will be evaluated before the function a is called.

To this list of five guarantees, C adds one more sequence guarantee:

```
6.  each full expression
```

C guarantees that each *full expression* (the enclosing expression that is not a subexpression) will be evaluated completely before going further.

The five operators above, plus the "full expression", are the "sequence points" of C++, the guarantees of sequential execution.

Commas, when used to separate arguments in a function invocation, are *not operators*, and no evaluation order should be assumed. Only the *operator* comma will guarantee order of evaluation, as in this example:

```
tmp = x[i], x[i] = x[j], x[j] = tmp;
```

Code which depends on the order of evaluation may perform differently with different compilers or different machines, may perform differently when the code generator for a given compiler is changed at some future time, and may even perform differently with the same compiler if changes to the program affect the allocation of registers.

These sequencing properties become second-nature to the experienced
C and C++ programmer. If the sequenced operators (comma,&&, ||, ?:)
are overloaded, however, they lose their sequencing properties. Don't
overload them.

EXAMPLE

```
if (j < MAXBOUND && a[j] == TARGET) // ok order-dependence

printf("%d:%d\\n", ++i, ++i); // bad order-dependence
```

[LOCAL NOTES]

TOPIC: 2.07 parens - parentheses

STANDARD

Bitwise operators (& | ^ >> <<) should be explicitly parenthesized when combined with other medium-precedence operators (arithmetic, bitwise, relational, logical):

```
if ((status & MASK) != SET)
    field = (w >> OFFSET) | FLAG;
```

The embedded assignment operator must also be explicitly parenthesized in these same contexts, because of its lower precedence:

```
while ((c = getchar()) != EOF)
    ++nc;
```

For the other operators, a competent C++ programmer should be expected to know the precedence rules of the language, and not to insert needless parentheses routinely.

JUSTIFICATION

The precedence of bitwise operators is intrinsically ambiguous. In certain respects, they behave like arithmetic operators, producing quasi-arithmetic results. In other respects, they are like logical operators, producing a "yes-or-no" result. The simplest course is always to use parentheses with bitwise operators.

The precedence of the pointer-to-member operators is somewhat counter-intuitive. They are similar to the high-precedence "dot" and "arrow" operators, but they are just above multiplication in precedence. In their non-overloaded form, they seldom cause problems because the right-hand operand must be a pointer-to-member, so incorrect grouping will usually be caught by the compiler. But if they ever are overloaded, use explicit parentheses, as in (p.*q)().

When these less-common operators are excluded from consideration, the precedence of the other operators is natural and intuitive. The following five mnemonic rules are common, fluent C++ constructs:

         Copyright © 1991, Thomas Plum and Dan Saks

a = -b + c[d]	primary and unary are obviously strongest
a + b < c + d	arithmetic is naturally stronger than relational
a < b && c < d	relational is stronger than logical
a = b ? c : d	a conditional can be assigned to something
a = b, c = d	assignments can be strung together with commas

Also remember that multiplicative arithmetic operators (* / %) are stronger than additive arithmetics (+ -), and that the multiplicative logical (&&) is stronger than the additive logical (||).

All these rules, when taken together, specify the precedence of C++ is a mnemonic way:

PRECEDENCE LEVEL	MNEMONIC EXAMPLE
primary	
unary	a = -b + c[d]
arithmetic (multiplicative)	
arithmetic (additive)	
relational	a + b < c + d
logical (multiplicative)	a < b && c < d
logical (additive)	
conditional	a = b ? c : d
assignments	
comma	a = b, c = d

[LOCAL NOTES]

TOPIC: 2.08 rightshift - right-shift and unsigned data

STANDARD

Always cast the left-hand operand of right-shift to an unsigned type, in portable code.

JUSTIFICATION

Sign-extension is either compiler-dependent or machine-dependent. Also, right-shift as "pseudo-divide" can give wrong results for negative numbers.

EXAMPLE

```
mask = ~0 >> n;          // bad - can give -1 result for any n

mask = ~(uint)0 >> n;  // good - guarantees unsigned shift
```

[LOCAL NOTES]

[LOCAL NOTES]

TOPIC: 2.09 sideorder - order of side effects

STANDARD

Programs must not depend upon the order in which side effects take place. In particular, the postfix increment/decrement operators may alter the memory at unpredictable times during the evaluation of the expression. All that C guarantees is that the side effect will be complete when the next "sequence point" is reached (see Section 2.06).

Here is a simplistic but useful rule: a variable which is the operand of increment, decrement, or embedded assignment should not have any more appearances in the same arithmetic expression.

Here is a more complex, but automatable, rule from the ANSI/ISO C Standard: do not write any expression in which an unordered operator contains in one operand a side-effect to an lvalue, where the other operand contains either an access or a side-effect to the same lvalue.

JUSTIFICATION

Programs that depend upon the order of side effects may not perform correctly when ported to a new machine or a new compiler.

EXAMPLE

```
a[i] = i++;      // bad - which is done first?  [] or ++ ?

++i + i // bad - is i changed before second i is accessed?

n = (i = 2) + i + 5;           // bad - i appears twice

s[i++] = t[j++];      // good - does not depend upon order
```

[LOCAL NOTES]

       Copyright © 1991, Thomas Plum and Dan Saks

[LOCAL NOTES]

TOPIC: 2.10 conv - conversions and overflow

STANDARD

Do not depend upon the returned value from the math functions for detecting errors. Create a project-wide inquiry function such as `test_math_err(x)`, which examines (a) the argument x, and (b) any global error indicator such as `errno`, to tell whether any math errors have occurred. Create a reset function such as `reset_math_error()` to clear any previous errors. (See Section 6.2.)

Or, if possible, prevent math errors by carefully bounds-checking before calling functions. In particular, the following domain errors should be prevented by prior bounds-checking:

```
Function              Bounds-checking
acos(x), asin(x)      -1 <= x  && x <= 1
atan2                 x != 0  ||  y != 0
log, log10            x >= 0
pow(x, y)             x != 0  ||  y >= 0
sqrt(x)               x >= 0
```

The calling function should take alternative action if these bounds are violated.

When two `unsigned int`'s are subtracted, convert the result using either `(uint)` or `(int)`.

Create an "integer modulus" function (or some similar mechanism) to ensure that a non-negative modulo result is produced. (See an example `imod` function in Section 4.20.)

In (signed) integer arithmetic, assume that overflow is invalid behavior, may be detected (hence should never be programmed), and cannot be trapped or ignored. Program in a style that prevents integer overflow.

ALTERNATIVES

In (signed) integer arithmetic, the default assumption of most existing C environments is that integer overflow is silently ignored. A project which does not foresee integer overflow trapping in its future environment may wish to allow silent overflows in project code, provided that integer expression limits are enforced with explicit tests. (See Section 5.5.)

[LOCAL NOTES]

[LOCAL NOTES]

TOPIC: 2.11 ctype - character tests

STANDARD

Use the <ctype.h> facilities for character tests and upper-lower conversions: `isalnum`, `isalpha`, `iscntrl`, `isdigit`, `isgraph`, `islower`, `isprint`, `ispunct`, `isspace`, `isupper`, `isxdigit`, `tolower`, `toupper`.

JUSTIFICATION

These facilities are portable across different character code sets, are usually very efficient, and promote international flexibility.

Note, however, that other similarly-named functions (such as `_tolower`, `_toupper`, `isascii`) are not universally portable.

EXAMPLE

```
if ('a' <= c && c <= 'z')
        // bad - assumes that letters are contiguous

if (islower(c))
        // good - portable to different character sets,
        // even non-English sets with extra letters
```

[LOCAL NOTES]

[LOCAL NOTES]

TOPIC: 3.01 loopscope - scope of loop variable

STANDARD

Whenever a `for` statement is the single-statement body of an enclosing control construct (`if`, `while`, `for`, or `do`), and the `for` initialization is a declaration, the `for` statement should be enclosed in braces.

EXAMPLE

```
while (j > 0)
    for (int k = 0; k < n; ++k)      // BAD - versions of C++ differ
        f(k);                        //       re scope and semantics
while (j > 0)
    {
    for (int k = 0; k < n; ++k)      // OK - no uncertainties about
        f(k);                        //       scope or semantics
    }
```

JUSTIFICATION

There have been differing treatments of the scope and semantics of single-`for`-statement bodies in various versions of the C++ Reference Manual, various drafts of the ANSI C++ standard, and various implementations. The scope of the declared name (`k`, here) is handled differently in different versions, and in some versions the "BAD" version gives a syntax error. Using the braces eliminates the version uncertainties, and also makes the scope of the name visually clear.

We also justify this rule on grounds of reliability. It is a good example of avoiding surprises in "programming-in-the-large" even if the source file grows by two extra lines for the braces. Following this style rule eliminates an uncertainty.

Note that this is similar in appearance and purpose to the requirement that a nested `if` statement must be enclosed in braces, to avoid the `else`-matching ambiguity.

[LOCAL NOTES]

[LOCAL NOTES]

TOPIC: 3.02 while - while and the N+1/4 - time loop

STANDARD

Side effects are explicitly allowed in the test of `while` or `for`. The underlying flow chart shows a box that is executed N+1 times whenever the lower box is executed N times, so the loop is known as an "N+1/2 - time" loop. The upper box is only an expression, whereas the lower box is an entire statement, so the loop can be called an "N+1/4 - time" loop.

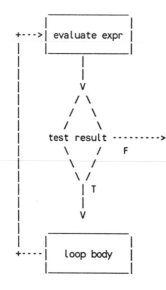

JUSTIFICATION

Such side effects are one of the *strengths* of C and C++; they smoothly handle a large proportion of common loops. They almost eliminate the awkward "duplicated read" loops, yet they require no complicated "lookahead" mechanism.

[LOCAL NOTES]

[LOCAL NOTES]

TOPIC: 3.03 loopinvar – designing with loop invariants

GUIDELINE

The "invariant condition" of a loop is a "typical picture" of the loop variables, a relationship which

      o   is always true at each iteration of the loop, and still true at loop termination; and

      o   guarantees that the goal of the loop is attained when the loop terminates.

Consider this familiar loop:

```
while ((c = getchar()) != EOF)
    putchar(c);
```

The invariant condition is "A series of n characters have been read and already printed out in sequence, and one more character c has been read but not yet printed." This condition is true at the start of the loop; and if it is true for n iterations, after we go around the loop once more, it becomes true for $n+1$. The condition guarantees that the goal of the loop is attained at termination, because when c is EOF, all the characters from beginning to end of file have been read and printed.

Graphically, this invariant condition, or "typical picture" looks like this:

```
Already read:       _ _ ... _ _
                              c

Already printed:    _ _ ... _
```

There may be portions of the loop body during which this "typical picture" is not true (as the variables are altered). For example, in the getchar loop above, the picture is not strictly true just after c is printed and just before getchar delivers the new c. These portions are the "domain of exceptions".

The program will be *more readable* if the *domain of exceptions is minimized*.

[LOCAL NOTES]

[LOCAL NOTES]

JUSTIFICATION

Altering the relationship between variables during a loop increases the complexity of the reader's task. The more complex the loop, the greater the need for this uniformity.

"Minimizing the domain of exceptions" gives an explicit justification for the experienced programmer's intuition that certain forms of for loops are preferable; they confine the domain of exceptions to the for line.

EXAMPLE

```
for (p = head; p != NULL; p = p->next)
    {
    /* invariant - p points to current item for processing */
    ... process p
    }

for (pp = &head; *pp && (*pp)->next; pp = &(*pp)->next)
    {
    /* invariant -
     *  *pp is pointer to current item, and
     *  (*pp)->next is pointer to the item after it;
     *  insert/delete can be done by altering *pp;
     *  both are non-NULL
     */
    ... process *pp and (*pp)->next
    }
```

[LOCAL NOTES]

[LOCAL NOTES]

TOPIC: 3.04 elseif - multiple-choice constructs

STANDARD

The else-if should be used for multiple-choice constructs whenever the conditions are not mutually exclusive, whenever their order of evaluation is important, or whenever they test different variables. Otherwise, use the switch.

Do not make up artificial variables just to make use of a switch.

In either case, each alternative action is tabbed to the same indent.

In a switch, each group of statements should end with a break before the next case label. In unusual cases, it is allowable for one group of statements to "flow-through" into the next label, but a standard comment such as

```
/* flow-through */
```

must appear in place of the break.

ALTERNATIVES

In addition to the rules above, each switch can be required to specify an explicit (possibly empty) default case. Some projects have found this useful for bug-prevention.

JUSTIFICATION

Although the else-if could always be used instead of switch, the distinction is helpful for readability. The efficiency of switch is sometimes significant. The indentation shows the logical nature of the multiple-choice.

EXAMPLE

```
if (!legal(code))
    remark("bad code: ", code);
else if (lookup(code))
    remark("multiple definition: ", code);
else
    install(code, val);
```

```
switch (sc)
    {
case EXTERN:
    remark("redefined", "");
    break;
case LOCAL:
    osc = LOCAL;
    /* flow-through */
case STATIC:
    printf("...");
    break;
case INTERN:
    printf("...");
    sc = STATIC;
    break;
default:
    remark("unknown sc", "");
    }
```

[LOCAL NOTES]

TOPIC: 3.05 control – restrictions on control structures

STANDARD

The goto statement (and hence labels as well) should not be used.

The while loop should be used instead of the do-while loop, except where the logic of the problem explicitly requires doing the body at least once regardless of the loop condition.

If a single if-else can replace a continue, an if-else should be used.

JUSTIFICATION

The goto statement is prohibited for the empirical reason that its use is highly correlated with errors and hard-to-read code, and for the abstract reason that algorithms should be expressed in structures that facilitate checking the program against the structure of the underlying process. (See Section 3.06 for detailed explanation; see Section 0.01 regarding occasional exceptions.)

The do-while is discouraged because loops should be coded in such a form as to "do nothing gracefully"; i.e. they should test their looping condition before executing the body.

[LOCAL NOTES]

[LOCAL NOTES]

TOPIC: 3.06 structure - program structure and problem structure

GUIDELINE

The structure of the data being processed (expressed in augmented BNF — "Backus Normal Form"— or equivalent notation) should match the structure of the program.

Sequence:

If the data structure is

   a   b   c

(which means "items *a*, *b*, and *c* in that order") the program structure will be a sequence, such as

```
process a; process b; process c;
```

Choice:

If the data structure is

   a | b

(which means "choice between *a* or *b*") the program structure will be a conditional, such as

```
if (data is a)
    process a;
else
    process b;
```

Repetition:

If the problem structure is

   a❋

(which means "repetition of the item *a*") the program structure will be a loop, such as

```
while (more a)
    process a;
```

or

```
for (first a; more a; next a)
    process a;
```

JUSTIFICATION

The usefulness of syntax-oriented design has been well-established in practice. Writing down the data syntax helps get the problem clear.

The data syntax gives a reliable outline for the first draft of the program. And the process of checking the resulting program against the data syntax aids in the review.

EXAMPLE

Data structure is

$$\{\, a \mid b \mid c \,\}*$$

(which means "a repetition of a choice among a, b, and c")

Program structure is

```
while (get an item)
    {
    if (its type is A)
        process type-A code;
    else if (its type is B)
        process type-B code;
    else if (its type is C)
        process type-C code;
    else
        error("invalid code: ", code);
    }
```

[LOCAL NOTES]

TOPIC: 4.01 codemgt - code management

GUIDELINE

This guideline is primarily addressed to projects which develop components for immediate application into one specific project, with a secondary objective of producing classes for re-use in subsequent projects.

Place class declarations in header files. A given header may contain the declarations for several closely related classes. For example, the header for a linked-list class should contain the declaration for the linked-list node class. That header may also contain the declaration for a list iterator class.

A class header should include all inline function definitions for the classes its declares, after the class declaration, not within it. (This way, functions can more easily be moved into or out of inline status.) It may also include const definitions and extern declarations (without initializers). The header should not include any non-inline function definitions, nor any static data member definitions or initializers.

Place the non-inline methods (function members) declared in a single header in a single source file. For example, if a single header contains the declarations for a list, list node, and list iterator, then all of the non-inline methods for those classes should be in a single source file. The source file should also contain the initializers for any static data member of the classes.

If a given source file contains many methods, but only a few will be used in a typical application, then arrange the file so that it can be "fractured". Fracturing a source file compiles each method into a separate object file. The object files are then collected into an object library. There are two simple techniques for fracturing source files.

The first technique is to place a conditional compilation "wrapper" around each method. For example,

```
#ifdef XXX

void X::foo()
    {
    // ...
    }

#endif
```

Use a different symbol in place of xxx for each conditional. The symbol could be an encoding of the function name and its arguments, similar to the name "mangling" scheme used internally by many C++ translators. A simpler alternative is to use sequentially numbered symbols, like X01, X02, etc. To compile a single method separately, define one of the conditional symbol on the compiler command line. For example,

```
CC -DX02 -osource02.o source.c
```

compiles the second method of source.c into an object file x02.o.

Another technique for fracturing is to implement a simple fracturing tool that writes each method to a separate source file. The fracturing tool relies on special comments inserted into the source to determine the fracturing points. For example,

```
// common

const int N = 10;

// fracture

void X::foo()
    {
    // ...
    }

// fracture

void X::bar()
    {
    // ...
    }

// fracture
// common
```

The tool writes each "fracture" section to a separate file with a unique name. The "common" sections contain code that's copied to each fractured file. Each separate source file may be erased after compilation.

JUSTIFICATION

Most C++ translators translate a single source file into a single object module. If any method in the object module is linked into a program, all of the methods in that module are also linked, even if they are not used by the program. This increases the program's size unnecessarily. (Although more sophisticated linkers do all this work automatically, they aren't universally available.)

Placing all the methods and static data objects in a single file avoids file naming problems for overloaded functions and operators. For example, if each of the String operators

```
String &String::operator =(const String &);
String &String::operator +=(const String &);
friend String &operator +(const String &, const String &);
```

were in a separate file, what unique file name would you use for each function, especially on systems like MS-DOS which limit file names to eight characters? If you use only one file, then you simply use the class name as the file name (with the appropriate extension).

The primary disadvantage of fracturing is that it renders the dependency checking in a *make* system useless. A change to any method in the source file forces recompilation of all methods. Therefore, avoid fracturing during development of the application at hand, and only fracture the class when preparing it for widespread distribution.

ALTERNATIVES

Coggins and Bollella (1989) describe a strategy for managing a large hierarchical library. Each non-inline member is placed in a separate source file. Each source file name is generated from an encoding of the function name. All source files for a class are placed in a common subdirectory. The source files for a derived class are placed in a subdirectory of the base class.

Some environments may preclude the use of inline functions, such as persistent-object database environments, or projects attempting to minimize re-compilations (Section 6.11).

[LOCAL NOTES]

[LOCAL NOTES]

TOPIC: 4.02 const - referencing unmodified arguments

STANDARD

When a function parameter is a pointer or a reference, and the function does not modify the object referenced, the parameter should always be declared as a pointer-to-const or reference-to-const.

EXAMPLE

```
size_t strlen(const char *str); /* OK - accepts any string */

char *strcpy(char *s1, const char *s2);
                        /* OK - modifies  s1 , but not  s2 */
```

JUSTIFICATION

This allows the function to receive both constant and non-constant arguments. Both reliability and efficiency are improved.

[LOCAL NOTES]

[LOCAL NOTES]

TOPIC: 4.03 defarg - default arguments

GUIDELINE

Use default arguments to shorten a function's calling sequence for common special cases. For example,

```
istream &istream::get(char *, int, char = '\n');
    // delimiter for sequence of input chars is often '\n'
```

permits the function to be called with only two arguments, as in

```
while (cin.get(buf, sizeof(buf))
```

Use default arguments to combine several overloaded functions into one. For example,

```
complex::complex();             // real and imag parts are zero
complex::complex(double);       // explicit real; imag part is zero
complex::complex(double, double);  // explicit real and imag parts
```

can be implemented as just

```
complex::complex(double = 0, double = 0);
```

However, do not eliminate the default constructors for a class x

```
X::X()
```

if arrays of X are permitted.

Declarations containing default arguments should appear at file scope, not inside a function. Compilers differ in their treatment.

JUSTIFICATION

Specifying sensible default argument values makes function calls shorter and more readable. Adding default values to existing arguments doesn't alter the generated code in the function body, and adds no overhead to a function call. A single function with default arguments is shorter and more maintainable than several overloaded functions with nearly identical implementations.

Combining overloaded inline functions into one with default arguments usually doesn't change the code generated by a call. For example, the default constructor for complex can be defined as

```
inline complex::complex() : re(0), im(0) { }
```

or as

```
inline complex::complex(double r = 0, double i = 0)
    : re(r), im(i) { }
```

In either way, the declaration

```
complex c1;
```
generates
```
c1.re = 0;
c1.im = 0;
```
Collapsing several out-of-line functions into one with default arguments reduces the object code occupied by the function definitions by eliminating entire functions.

ALTERNATIVES

Replacing an out-of-line function with a similar function with additional default arguments increases the code generated for each call. For example, given
```
void foo(int);
void foo(int, int);
```
then call such as foo(3) generates code to pass only one argument. If the two functions are combined as one
```
void foo(int, int = 0);
```
then the same call, foo(3), generates additional code to pass the default value of the second argument. If this increase in the code size and execution time for a call is unacceptable, don't combine overloaded functions into a single function with default arguments.

E&S (1990) states that a constructor with all default arguments is a default constructor. That is,
```
X::X(int = 0);
```
can be used just like
```
X::X();
```
in constructing arrays of objects. However, many 1991-vintage C++ compilers do not accept this alternative. It is only a minor nuisance to continue writing default constructors explicitly with no arguments.

[LOCAL NOTES]

137

TOPIC: 4.04 globinit - initialization of global objects

GUIDELINE

Objects in static storage which are initialized to non-constant expressions and/or have a constructor are initialized in the order that they appear in the source file.

If possible, avoid depending upon the order of initialization of statics; it adds complexity to the design.

When several static objects are declared in several source files, and an object of class A must be initialized before any objects of class B can be initialized, a coding technique ("trick") is needed to ensure that the initializations take place in the right order. The description below is summarized from Jerry Schwarz's definitive article "Initializing Static Variables in C++ Libraries".

The trick is to declare, in the header for object A's type, an initialization class with a static counter. Use of the counter ensures that actual initialization takes place on the first execution of the constructor for the initialization class, and that the actual destruction takes place at the last execution of the destructor for the initialization class.

In the header for class A:

```
class A { friend class A_init; /* members ... */ };
extern A *pA;     // declare, but don't define, a ptr-to-A
class A_init
    {
public:
    A_init();
    ~A_init();
private:
    static int init_count;    // shared by all A_init objects
    };
static A_init a_init_static;  // internal-linkage "file static"
```

In the source file for class A:

```
A *pA;                       // define pA
int A_init::init_count = 0;   // initialize the static counter
A_init::A_init()
    {
    if (++init_count > 1)
        return;              // already constructed
    pA = new A;
    // anything else needed to initialize the new A Object
    }
A_init::~A_init()
    {
    if (--init_count > 0)
        return;  // not ready to destroy yet
    // anything else needed to destroy the A Object
    delete pA;
    }
```

And in the header or source file that defines class B:

```
#include "A.h"
class B
    {
private:
    A a;
public:
    B() { /* ... */ };
    ~B() { /* ... */ };
    int j;
    };
```

Because "A.h" is included prior to any declarations of B objects, the internal-linkage ("file static") definition of a_init_static will appear prior to any initializations that want to refer to the A object (*pA). And the constructor for a_init_static will ensure that the A object has been initialized before those initializations want to see it.

For destructors, all the orderings are reversed.

JUSTIFICATION

Prefer simplicity but not at the cost of functionality.

REFERENCES

Ellis and Stroustrup [1990], Section 3.4.

Jerry Schwarz [1989], Pp 1-4.

[LOCAL NOTES]

TOPIC: 4.05 preproc - minimizing use of preprocessor

GUIDELINE

For a variety of reasons, use of the preprocessor is generally discouraged in C++ work. Specifically:

Use enumerators or const declarations for integer constants, in preference to #define'd macro constants:

```
enum {MAXROW=24};        // OK - can be used for any integer
const int MAXROW = 24;   // OK - can be used for any constant
class Queue
    {
    enum {FULL, EMPTY};  // OK - scoped to class name
    /* ... */
    };
```

```
#define MAXROW 24        // bad (in general) - unscoped, unchecked
```

Use const declarations for non-integers, in preference to #define'd macro constants:

```
const double PI = acos(-1.);  // OK - scoped, better debugging
```

```
#define PI 3               // BAD - :-)
```

Use inline functions in preference to #define'd macro functions:

```
inline int min(int i, int j)
    {
    return i < j ? i : j;    // OK - no side-effect problems
    }
```

```
#define MIN(i, j) ((i)<(j)?(i):(j)) // BAD - "unprotected" side-effects
```

Use alternative class definitions for alternative environments —

```
/project/dos/lowlevel.h:
    class LowLevel
        {
        enum {EOF_CODE=032, /* ... */ };
        /* ... */
        };
```

```
/project/unix/lowlevel.h:
    class LowLevel
        {
        enum {EOF_CODE=004, /* ... */ };
        /* ... */
        };
```

in preference to #if conditional compilations:

```
#if MSDOS
    #define EOF_CODE 032
#elif UNIX
    #define EOF_CODE 004
#endif
```

On the other hand: As of 1991, there are specific uses of the preprocessor that have no convenient alternative. Sophisticated schemes of re-naming and name-catenation require #define. There is no portable alternative to #if for conditional inclusion/exclusion of situation-dependent cases. (Names to be tested by #if must, of course, be #define'd macro names, not enumerators or const values.) The use of "#ifdef __cplusplus" allows us to maintain one source file for both C and C++ uses. And the "#ifdef HEADER_H ... #endif" wrapper around header-file contents has become a widely-used construct.

Therefore, use the preprocessor when it solves the problem at hand. To facilitate eventual incremental compilation, do not #undef anything. Do not depend upon the exact value of the __LINE__ macro. Ensure that each macro expands into all or part of one syntactic entity — one identifier, one constant, one expression, or one statement. That is, do not write macros which complete one entity and start another, such as this attempt to make C (or C++) resemble Algol:

```
#define IF    if (      /* BAD - crosses syntax boundary */
#define THEN  ) {       /* BAD - crosses syntax boundary */
#define ELSE  } else {  /* BAD - crosses syntax boundary */
#define FI    }         /* ... (well, not a problem by itself) */
```

JUSTIFICATION

Reader, be warned that this topic is fraught with all the doctrinaire fervor that once characterized the C debate over "where do the braces go" and the structured-methodology debate over "is a global variable ever justified".

Influential software veterans have seen widespread maintainability problems with undisciplined uses of the preprocessor. The end result is that use of the preprocessor is widely stigmatized, much as the use of interactive debuggers was stigmatized by the early fans of structured programming.

To be sure, there are some practical advantages to using language features rather than macros. Syntax-checking is better. Preprocessor names cut across all block-scope boundaries, with no regard for good scope or access restrictions. Debuggers can more accurately display enum or const values than #define'd macro names. Inline functions are easier to write correctly than are macro functions.

Eventually, some day, vendors may provide integrated environments with incremental compilation. Such environments would be easier to produce if the programs they compile avoided use of the preprocessor. But the history of Instant-C, a commercial incremental compiler for C, shows that almost all preprocessor constructs can actually be handled by an incremental compiler.

[LOCAL NOTES]

[LOCAL NOTES]

TOPIC: 4.06 headers – project-wide standard headers

STANDARD

All programs within a project should use a locally-written header designed for use by that project; this file is generically referred to as local.h in this book. This file should declare, include, define, and typedef everything of general usefulness for the project.

Using a local standard header can allow portable code to be compiled for different environments. The environment-dependent definitions in the header may have to change, but the source code of the application will not have to change.

There should be one designated header directory (or a small list of directories) for each project. Each header can then be accessed in the project header directory.

All definitions of compile-time values and of structure formats should be put into headers if they are shared by more than one file.

Reliable modification of defined constants requires an environmental capability: there must be a means for ensuring that all files comprising a program have been compiled using the same set of headers. (The UNIX make command is one such capability.)

JUSTIFICATION

The choice of header environments requires some skill and experience, and is often best made by team leaders or senior programmers. The inclusion of a single local.h file is then easier for standardization than the specification of a list of #include's and #define's. Rigorous use of #ifndef...#endif sandwiches around headers (see Section 4.10) will eliminate the most common objection to project-wide headers, namely that they make multiply-included files more likely.

The names defined in project-wide headers (either directly or via nested #include) are, in effect, reserved words for that project; even if a programmer makes no use of some group of names, later modifications to the program might introduce them. Name conflicts should be discovered early if possible.

Different versions of a project can have different #include environments without introducing problems of retroactively modifying existing code.

Functions must be declared before being called. Putting each function declaration into an associated header is the most reliable way.

ALTERNATIVES

Programs for general publication (in articles or newsletters) should use a minimal set of generally-available headers. Only these headers provided by C++ and Standard C should be assumed in general-publication programs:

```
<new.h>, <iostream.h>  (C++)

<assert.h>, <ctype.h>, <errno.h>, <float.h>,
<limits.h>, <locale.h>, <math.h>, <setjmp.h>,
<signal.h>, <stdarg.h>, <stddef.h>, <stdio.h>,
<stdlib.h>, <string.h>, <time.h>  (C)
```

[LOCAL NOTES]

TOPIC: 4.07 files - size of source files

STANDARD

Source files should be no larger than 500 lines.

JUSTIFICATION

Experience has shown that larger files are cumbersome to edit correctly and to maintain.

ALTERNATIVES

On large mainframe systems, a more commonly-used limit is 1000 lines.

[LOCAL NOTES]

[LOCAL NOTES]

TOPIC: 4.08 includes - put includes at head of file

STANDARD

Each source file should start with its list of #include's grouped at the head of the file, before any declarations or function definitions. After the #include's, next come any #define's needed for the file.

However, it may sometimes be necessary for a #define to precede the #include's (to control conditional inclusion). Putting the #define first will emphasize that it affects the #include'd files.

JUSTIFICATION

Headers form the context for the code in the file. Grouping them together allows quick verification of the list, and facilitates any necessary dependency-checking.

EXAMPLE

```
#include "local.h"
#include "specific.h"

#define GOODCODE 1
#define BADCODE 0
// now comes the rest of the program
```

[LOCAL NOTES]

[LOCAL NOTES]

TOPIC: 4.09 stdflags - standard compile-time flags

STANDARD

Standard compile-time flags should be chosen project-wide for environmental issues such as target machine, target operating system, and debug options. Such flags should not be hard-coded into the program (unless required by its environment-specific function), because they can be turned on by command line option.

JUSTIFICATION

Judiciously chosen conditional definitions allow efficient targeting of such issues as word size, byte size, and specific forms for system interfaces such as file control blocks, etc. Selective trace and assertion functions can be included with ease if a flag such as NDEBUG is available to turn off code production when not wanted.

[LOCAL NOTES]

[LOCAL NOTES]

TOPIC: 4.10 nest - nested headers

STANDARD

To avoid multiple inclusions of the contents of a header, each header should begin with a `#ifndef` that tests whether some `#define`'d symbol has already been defined, and should end with `#endif`.

Each header should `#include` any other headers whose definitions are assumed. If possible, the header should test, with `#ifndef`, whether the `#include` is necessary.

JUSTIFICATION

The contents of each header should be included only once during each compilation. If the `#include`'s are nested unconditionally, this property becomes hard to control.

Making the `#include` itself to be conditional can improve the speed of compilations.

EXAMPLE

```
local.h:

    #ifndef LOCAL_H
    #define LOCAL_H

    #ifndef BUFSIZ
    #include <stdio.h>
    #endif

    ... other definitions

    #endif
```

[LOCAL NOTES]

[LOCAL NOTES]

TOPIC: 4.11 noinit - no initializations in headers

STANDARD

Headers should not contain initialization of anything.

JUSTIFICATION

Putting the initialization in a header doesn't make clear which function "owns" the data; i.e., it doesn't localize the "defining instance".

Multiple source files each including a file containing initializations will, in general, produce "multiply defined" diagnostics.

In general, programmers should be assured that #include'ing various headers will not increase their object-code size.

[LOCAL NOTES]

[LOCAL NOTES]

TOPIC: 4.12 coupling - methods of coupling modules together

STANDARD

Data that is to be shared by two functions should be local (external static) unless global linkage is specifically necessary.

Minimize coupling between unrelated functions.

In procedural designs, this means that the preferred method for cross-function communication is the passing of arguments. However, "pass-through" parameters, whose only function is to pass data downward to called functions, create a problem for both readability and maintainability. If two or more levels of pass-through are required, use either external data or "package" modules. Also, certain data of an "environmental" or "context" nature is more conveniently handled as a "default" value. For example, the standard I/O functions (getchar, putchar, printf, etc.) make use of globally-known values for stdin and stdout. The mechanism to override the default is also available (getc, putc, fprintf, etc.) for cases in which the default is not appropriate.

In object-based designs, minimizing coupling also means restricting access to the internal representation of objects. Use member functions to access objects.

JUSTIFICATION

Integration problems are made more probable by each global linkage.

[LOCAL NOTES]

[LOCAL NOTES]

TOPIC: 4.13 cohesion - cohesion and meaningful functions

STANDARD

A function should evidence "functional cohesiveness" (Yourdon and Constantine, 1978), which can be adequately summarized by the following test:

> Can the purpose of the function be accurately summarized by a sentence in the form
>
> > "specific verb + specific object(s)"?

This sentence should appear in a comment just before the function.

This criterion is as relevant to member functions as it is to procedural functions. However, good "verbish" names for member functions, and good "nounish" names for parameters should make the one-sentence comment redundant for member functions.

JUSTIFICATION

The logic of the calling module can be verified only if the action of each called function can be grasped without having to resort to line-by-line reading.

[LOCAL NOTES]

[LOCAL NOTES]

TOPIC: 4.14 libfns - file structure for procedural library functions

STANDARD

General-purpose functions (i.e., functions callable by more than one main) should be placed in separate source files.

General-purpose functions must be documented and maintained as library functions, including a manual-page specification.

Each such file should contain at its end a main function which will try out the called function. This test driver should be surrounded by a #ifdef and #endif keyed to a compilation flag (e.g., TRYMAIN) chosen project-wide.

In portable programs, the names of the Standard C Library functions should be treated as reserved words. In other words, do not make a new function named fopen, even if its behavior is supposed to mimic the Standard fopen function.

JUSTIFICATION

Object files are created on a per-source-file basis. Calling programs should not inadvertently link multiple functions when they need only one function.

Standardizing the format of tryout functions and putting them into the source reduces the number of files to be maintained and places examples of use in a place where they are most likely to be seen.

ALTERNATIVES

See Section 4.01 regarding a "fracturing tool" to collect individual functions into a single source file, compile them into separate object files, and collect them into an object library.

EXAMPLE

This example illustrates possible source code for the Standard C
Library function strcmp, which is obliged to use unsigned comparisons.
(For the rationale behind the choice of test cases, see Section 8.01.)

```
/* strcmp - compare (unsigned) strings */
int strcmp(
    register const char s[],  /* : string */
    register const char t[])  /* : string */
    {
    typedef unsigned char uchar;

    while (*s != '\0' && *s == *t)
        {
        ++s;
        ++t;
        }
    if (*(uchar *)s < *(uchar *)t)
        return -1;
    else if (*(uchar *)s == *(uchar *)t)
        return 0;
    else
        return 1;
    }
#ifdef TRYMAIN
#include <limits.h>
#include <assert.h>
#undef NDEBUG   /* turn on assert's */
char s_max[2] = {UCHAR_MAX, '\0'};  /* string with largest uchar */
int main()
    {
    assert(strcmp("", s_max) < 0);  /* case 1 */
    assert(strcmp("a", "a") == 0);  /* case 2 */
    assert(strcmp(s_max, "") > 0);  /* case 3 */
    exit(0);
    }
#endif
```

[LOCAL NOTES]

TOPIC: 4.15 portlib - use of portable library

STANDARD

A portable program interacts with its environment through the class and library interfaces that are chosen by the project. Other than these capabilities, a portable program should not assume anything else about its environment.

At the outset, determine the intended future range of target environments. Then stay within that range:

> Do not assume system-specific I/O formats.

> Do not assume availability of system commands.

> Do not assume system-specific command-invocations.

The streams `cin`, `cout`, and `cerr` are provided by `<iostream.h>` (or in older environments, `<stream.h>`.) The files `stdin`, `stdout`, and `stderr` are provided by the Standard C Library.

`cin, stdin`	standard input (should be meaningful for file or terminal)
`cout, stdout`	standard output (either file or terminal)
`cerr, stderr`	standard error output (where all error messages should be sent)

JUSTIFICATION

Occasional use "for convenience" of handy system-specific functions may create serious portability problems later. The new system may not have the same formats or commands as the old system.

[LOCAL NOTES]

[LOCAL NOTES]

TOPIC: 4.16 fnsize - suggested size of functions

GUIDELINE

Programs should be designed so that most of the functions will be smaller than 50 lines of source listing. When properly designed, most member functions should be considerably smaller.

This guideline does not require artificial splitting of cohesive code into small pieces.

On the other hand, code which consists of nothing but large-function files usually reveals insufficient attention to design prior to launching into code.

JUSTIFICATION

Algorithms are easier to create and to understand if they are built of pieces small enough to be grasped as one concept.

The 50-line guideline is derived from empirical observation of well-crafted C code.

ALTERNATIVES

Most member functions should fit onto one display screen, e.g. 20 lines of source code.

[LOCAL NOTES]

[LOCAL NOTES]

TOPIC: 4.17 macros – writing macros

STANDARD

In Typesafe C, macros are used for a variety of purposes. In Object-Based C++, and Full C++, macros are needed only for testing by #if and for representing complicated constant expressions. (See Section 4.05.)

A "protected" macro is fully parenthesized and evaluates each argument exactly once, so it gives a result that is equivalent to a function call. These "protected" macros should be documented like functions, and given names in lower case.

"Unprotected" macros should be given names all in upper case.

When writing macros, be sure to put parentheses around the entire replacement text, to guard against operator precedence surprises. Also, each appearance of a parameter should have either parenthesis or comma on either side.

```
#define STREQ(s, t) (strcmp(s, t) == 0)    /* good */

#define SQUARE(x)   ((x) * (x))            /* good */
#define SQUARE(x)   x * x                  /* bad */

f = z / SQUARE(y + 1);
```

When documenting "unprotected" macros with a manual page, be sure to indicate a "NOTES" or "CAVEAT" entry, warning that the name is an "unprotected" macro and that no side effects should appear on its arguments.

JUSTIFICATION

The problems with side effects cause macros to behave differently from functions. The user must be protected when possible, and otherwise warned.

[LOCAL NOTES]

[LOCAL NOTES]

TOPIC: 4.18 stdarg - functions of a variable number of arguments

STANDARD

Functions should, in general, have a fixed number of arguments, each having a specified type.

In some exceptional situations, however, it is useful to create a function which has a variable number of arguments, or an argument of a varying type, or both. This is called a *variadic function*. The macros in <stdarg.h> should be used for all variadic functions.

JUSTIFICATION

In Typesafe C, this is the only portable way to handle varying numbers of arguments. It is also more readable than most system-specific methods.

ALTERNATIVES

In Object-Based C++ and Full C++, an alternative is to overload a binary operator to accept different types, such as is done in <iostream.h>:

```
cout << "x=" << x << '\n';
```

which replaces a call to the variadic printf:

```
printf("x=%d\n", x);
```

[LOCAL NOTES]

[LOCAL NOTES]

TOPIC: 4.19 ptrparms - pointer and reference parameters

STANDARD

The default requirement for pointer and reference parameters is that they must refer to storage that is entirely defined (i.e., not uninitialized garbage). Whenever a pointer or ref parameter can accept something else, this should be explicitly stated on that parameter's declaration comment.

The requirements depend upon the usage: "out-only" pointers and refs are used to modify memory, and not to inspect; "in-only" pointers and refs are used to inspect but not modify; "in-out" pointers and refs are used both to inspect and to modify.

Don't use out-only ref arguments; use a returned value, or a ref returned value, or an out-only pointer parameter. For in-only parameters, use a ref-to-const rather than a pointer-to-const. For in-out parameters, use a ref in preference to a pointer.

Regarding parameters which are pointers to class objects, an "out-only" pointer parameter is assumed to be non-null, pointing to the storage for a class object of the specified type. "In-only" and "in-out" pointer parameters are assumed to point to a well-defined class object of the specified type. Any exceptions should be noted in a comment on the parameter declaration.

Follow a consistent notation for pointer parameters. Either (1) declare all of them as *p (with the asterisk), or (2) use p[] for parameters designating arrays that do not overlap each other, and use *p for everything else.

JUSTIFICATION

The Plum Hall books follow the p[] convention for array-argument declarations, because it conveys important semantic information, because some new compilers reward this style with better optimization, and because it generalizes more gracefully to multi-dimensional arrays, such as p[] [10].

[LOCAL NOTES]

[LOCAL NOTES]

TOPIC: 4.20 headers - contents of local standard headers

GUIDELINE

This section will present the contents of the headers suggested for use in portable programs, besides those that are standard in C and C++.

The header portdefs.h (discussed in Section 1.17 and elsewhere) encapsulates the environment-dependent defined-types and macros:

```
/* portdefs.h - definitions for portability */
/* ENVIRONMENT-DEPENDENT - ADJUST TO LOCAL SYSTEM */
/* (Configured for use by C or C++ programs */
#ifndef PORTDEFS_H
#define PORTDEFS_H

#ifndef EXIT_SUCCESS
#include <stdlib.h> /* to get EXIT_* */
#endif

/* index_t - this type is chosen by the project */
typedef int             index_t;

/* the values for STDIN, STDOUT, STDERR (for file descriptors) */
/* are not part of Standard C, and may need to be changed */

#define STDIN        0
#define STDOUT       1
#define STDERR       2

/* NAM_LEN_EXTERNAL - length of external names */
#define NAM_LEN_EXTERNAL 31 /* could be reduced, even to 6 */

/* imod - modulo function giving non-negative result */
/* Replace with simple  i % j  if this is always non-negative */
#ifdef __cplusplus
inline int imod(int i, int j)
{ int m; if (j < 0) j = -j; m = i % j; if (m < 0) m += j; return m; }
inline long imod(long i, long j)
{ int m; if (j < 0) j = -j; m = i % j; if (m < 0) m += j; return m; }
#else
static long imod(long i, long j)
{ int m; if (j < 0) j = -j; m = i % j; if (m < 0) m += j; return m; }
#endif
```

```
/* STRICTEST_ALIGNMENT - which type has strictest alignment requirement */
typedef double STRICTEST_ALIGNMENT; /* adjust for each environment  */

/* the remaining definitions are the same for any C or C++ compiler  */
typedef signed char     schar;
typedef unsigned char   uchar;
typedef unsigned short  ushort;
typedef unsigned int    uint;
typedef unsigned long   ulong;
typedef int             bool;       /* could be char : bool  */
typedef short           metachar;   /* could be int : metachar  */

#endif /* PORTDEFS_H */
```

Some of these definitions will need adjustment to reflect the characteristics of each environment; they are grouped at the head of the file. The other definitions should be suitable for any Standard C environment.

As discussed in Section 4.06, the "local" standard header will #include a selection of Standard headers, to provide a uniform environment across different systems. The Standard C headers <assert.h>, <ctype.h>, <errno.h>, <float.h>, <limits.h>, <math.h>, <stddef.h>, <stdlib.h>, <stdio.h>, <string.h>, and <time.h> are included directly from the vendor-supplied Standard C headers. The C++ headers <new.h> and <iostream.h> (or alternatively <stream.h>) are included directly from the vendor-supplied C++ headers.

The Standard C headers <locale.h>, <setjmp.h>, <signal.h>, and <stdarg.h> are not suggested for use in the "local" standard header. They can be #include'd on an as-needed basis in each application.

Contents of the generic "local" header, local.h:

```
/* local.h - local standard header file  */
#ifndef LOCAL_H
#define LOCAL_H

#include <new.h>
#include <iostream.h>  /* change to  stream.h  if needed */

#ifndef assert
#include <assert.h>
#endif

#ifndef isalpha
#include <ctype.h>
#endif

#ifndef EDOM
#include <errno.h>
#endif

#ifndef DBL_MAX
#include <float.h>
#endif

#ifndef INT_MAX
#include <limits.h>
#endif

#ifndef HUGE_VAL
#include <math.h>
#endif

#ifndef offsetof
#include <stddef.h>
#endif

#ifndef EXIT_SUCCESS
#include <stdlib.h>
#endif

#ifndef BUFSIZ
#include <stdio.h>
#endif

#include <string.h>

#ifndef CLOCKS_PER_SEC
#include <time.h>
#endif
```

```
#define FALSE       0            /* : bool  */
#define NO          0            /* : bool  */
#define TRUE        1            /* : bool  */
#define YES         1            /* : bool  */
#define DIM(a)      (sizeof(a) / sizeof(a[0]))

#include "portdefs.h"   /* portability definitions  */

/* Add other project-selected definitions as required */
/* Also add definitions from prior Plum Hall versions as needed */

#endif  /* LOCAL_H  */
```

[LOCAL NOTES]

TOPIC: 5.01 lexdata - lexical rules for variables

STANDARD

Names of variables and functions should be written all in lower case. Use 31-character limits for all your names, internal and external. When porting to "deficient" environments in which linkers impose short name limits upon external symbols, each package's header file can #define long names into unique short names:

```
#include "portdefs.h"  // described in CPG 4.19_headers
#if NAM_LEN_EXTERNAL < 12
    #define data_base_update datab1
#endif
```

There is no reason intrinsic to C++ to require changes to the lexical layout rules that you have chosen for your work in C. There are, however, differences in emphasis and differences in "culture" that are worth considering.

For classes that provide a system-wide functionality analogous to built-in types and library functions, use all-lower-case names, as were chosen for complex and iostream. For other class names, capitalize each initial letter, as in ExampleClassName.

All names should be explicitly declared. Within each function, first come any register variable names (ordered by importance), and then the other names.

External names beginning with underscore should be reserved for the compiler or other systems programs, and should not be used in project code. Names that contain two underscores (anywhere) are also reserved, in C++.

Declarations should be written with only one variable per source line; however, when several uninitialized variables share the same type and properties, they may share a one-line declaration. Whenever a comment can add information, use it.

Brace-enclosed lists should be formatted with braces around each sub-aggregate, one row per line:

```
static short x[2][5] =
    {
    {1, 2, 3, 4, 5},
    {6, 7, 8, 9, 10},
    };
```

Variable name and type should be separated by single spaces, and descriptive comments should be attached at a lined-up position:

```
bool canhit;        // can player's hand take hit?
short tophand;      // how many hands is player playing : {1:2}
```

Each file-level declaration should be either a "definition" (without the keyword extern, and with an initializer) or a "referencing-declaration" (with the keyword extern, and no initializer). Storage class (if any) should precede the type specifier.

Do not put redundant parentheses around a declarator:

```
int (a)[5];  // BAD - misleading
int a[5];    // OK - no redundant parentheses

Type (c) = 7;  // BAD - misleading
Type c = 7;    // OK - no redundant parentheses
```

they confuse the reader, and they confuse some compilers.

When using the parenthesized initializer-list syntax, precede the parenthesized list with one space. The initializer list binds looser syntactically than all operators, so a space is consistent with the justification of operator spacing according to precedence. Without the space, the initialization visually resembles a function-call or function-like conversion.

```
Vector v (10);   // OK - space for low precedence
```

JUSTIFICATION

The rules pinpoint the location of declarations, avoid conflicts of upper- and lower-case names, and encourage documentation of the meaning of variable names.

The register variables are ordered for purposes of portable efficiency — compilers differ in the number of register requests honored.

ALTERNATIVES

In most C++ textbooks, parenthesized initializers are commonly preceded by no space.

```
Vector v(10);     // frequently used layout
```

[LOCAL NOTES]

       177

TOPIC: 5.02 lexops - lexical rules for operators

STANDARD

The primary operators "arrow" (->), "dot" (.), "scope resolution" (::), and "subscript" ([]) should be written with no space around them:

```
p->m   s.m   c::m   a[i]
```

Parentheses (another primary operator) after function names should have no space before them. Expressions within parentheses should be written with no space after the opening parenthesis and no space before the closing parenthesis:

```
exp(2., x)
```

The unary and postfix operators should also be written with no space between them and their operands:

```
!p   ~b   ++i   --j   -n   (long)m   *p   &x   sizeof(k)
```

The pointer-to-member operators should be written with no space between them and their operands:

```
s.*m   p->*m
```

The new and delete operators must be separated from adjacent names with a space (of course):

```
p = new int;
delete p;
```

But new and delete should not be placed into arbitrary expressions. Confine new to initialization or assignment. Confine delete to a statement of its own, as shown above.

The assignment operators should have space around them, and so should the conditional operator:

```
c1 = c2          i += j          n > 0 ? n : -n
```

Commas (and semicolons) should have one space (or newline) after them:

```
strncat(t, s, n)              for (i = 0; i < n; ++i)
```

The other operators should generally be written with one space on either side of the operator:

```
x + y          a < b && b < c    m + 1
```

Occasionally, these operators may appear with no space around them, but the operators with no space around them must bind their operands tighter than the adjacent operators:

```
flag ? a : b-10              printf(fmt, a+1, b+1, c+1)
```

To summarize this standard, we will classify the operators into high precedence (primary, unary, postfix, and pointer-to-member), low precedence (conditional, assignment, and comma), and medium precedence (all the others: pointer-to-member, arithmetic, bitwise, relational, logical). Using these categories, the high precedence operators never have space around them, the low precedence operators always have space around them, and the medium precedence operators usually have space around them. The new and delete operators require a space just because they are usually adjacent to another alphabetic name.

Keywords (if, while, for, switch, return) should be followed by one space.

JUSTIFICATION

Readability of the code is enhanced by a uniform layout of the operators.

Spaces are related to precedence by the following observation:

> Visually, spaces connote *looser binding* than the absence of spaces. Consider the difference in meaning between "light housekeeper" and "lighthouse keeper". The same principle labels this code as misleading:
>
> ```
> n = a+b * c;    /* bad - misleading spacing */
> ```

Automated processing of program text by editor programs and other text-searchers is possible only if spaces are rigorously formatted. Space after keywords allows easy visual distinction of control structures from function calls. Furthermore, in the syntax of C, keywords bind looser than all the operators.

[LOCAL NOTES]

179

TOPIC: 5.03 lexctl - lexical rules for control structure

STANDARD

Each source file that conforms to these standards is formatted consistently according to one of the following styles of bracing:

```
#1: indented braces      #2: exdented braces      #3: Kernighan & Ritchie

if (a == b)              if (a == b)              if (a == b) {
    {                    {                            err("b");
    err("b");                err("b");                ++nerrs;
    ++nerrs;                 ++nerrs;             }
    }                    }
```

However, an aggregate initializer which fits entirely on one line will usually have its opening and closing braces also on that line:

```
short a[] = {1, 1, 2, 3, 5};
```

Small functions, especially inlines, can appear all on one line. Such small functions can often replace the use of macro functions, and the one-line appearance encourages their use.

Small class definitions can appear all on one line. Slavish indentation would make the overall program too "tall and skinny", obscuring the real concepts.

All three bracing styles follow the same rule for the tabbing of subordinate lines: Each line which is part of the body of a C control structure (if, while, do-while, for, switch) is indented one tab stop from the margin of its controlling line. The same rule applies to function definitions, structure-or-union definitions, and aggregate initializers. (Examples in Plum Hall textbooks follow bracing style #1.)

Tabs should be reflected by a uniform amount of white space, preferably four spaces. Four is better than eight because the source listings do not tend to run off the right edge so quickly.

For code which contains no braces, the tabbing rules produce the same result:

```
if (a == 1)
    x = y;
```

```
if (a == b)
    ++nerrs;
else
    subfn(b);

if (root == 0)
    root = new treenode(w, n);
else if ((cond = strcmp(w, root->word)) == 0)
    root->lines.add(n);
else if (cond < 0)
    root->left.add(w, n);
else
    root->right.add(w, n);

while ((c = getchar()) != EOF)
    putchar(c);

for (;;)
    timetest(n);
```

Examples involving braces:

```
#1: indented braces      #2: exdented braces      #3: Kernighan & Ritchie
switch (tolower(opt))    switch (tolower(opt))
    {                    {                        switch (tolower(opt)) {
case 'b':                case 'b':                case 'b':
    bounds = TRUE;           bounds = TRUE;           bounds = TRUE;
    break;                   break;                   break;
case 'd':                case 'd':                case 'd':
    debug = TRUE;            debug = TRUE;            debug = TRUE;
    /* flow-through */       /* flow-through */       /* flow-through */
case 'v':                case 'v':                case 'v';
    verbose = TRUE;          verbose = TRUE;          verbose = TRUE;
    break;                   break;                   break;
default:                 default:                 default:
    usage();                 usage();                 usage();
    }                    }                        }

while (p != 0)           while (p != 0)
    {                    {                        while (p != 0) {
    ++syms;                  ++syms;                  ++syms;
    p = nxt(p);              p = nxt(p);              p = nxt(p);
    }                    }                        }

do                       do
    {                    {                        do {
    c = getans();            c = getans();            c = getans();
    } while (!ok(c));    } while (!ok(c));        } while (!ok(c));
```

```
struct item              struct item
    {                        {                        struct item {
    char *name;              char *name;                  char *name;
    char *value;             char *value;                 char *value;
    };                       };                       };

class line               class line
    {                        {                        class line {
public:                  public:                   public:
    void draw();             void draw();                 void draw();
private:                private:                  private:
    point a, b;;             point a, b;;              point a, b;;
    };                       };                       };
```

Nested control structures are formatted by the simple rule that the entire nested structure is indented to the margin of the surrounding body. For example:

```
while ((c = getchar()) != EOF)      /* #1: indented braces */
    {
    if (isspace(c))
        putchar('\n');
    else
        putchar(c);
    }

while ((c = getchar()) != EOF)      /* #2: exdented braces */
{
    if (isspace(c))
        putchar('\n');
    else
        putchar(c);
}

while ((c = getchar()) != EOF) {    /* #3: Kernighan & Ritchie */
    if (isspace(c))
        putchar('\n');
    else
        putchar(c);
}
```

Lines within a C source file should fit a listing (or screen) width of 80 characters. Any expression that is too long to fit this size should be broken into multiple lines. The proper place to break a line is at an operator of lower precedence than those that surround it.

A null statement appearing as the body of a control structure deserves a line of its own:

```
while (*s++ != '\0')
    ;
```

In the test expression of `while`, `for`, `do-while`, or `if`, the comparison should be written explicitly, rather than relying upon the default comparison to zero:

```
while (fgets(buf, BUFSIZ, stdin) != 0)
    process(buf);

if (system(cmd) != 0)
    fprintf(stderr, "cmd failed\n");
```

However, the comparison of `bool`'s to zero or non-zero is most legibly written without explicit comparison:

```
if (isspace(c))
    putchar('\n');
```

And comparison of characters to null characters, and pointers to null pointers, can be written as an implicit comparison, if a long or repetitive control line can be simplified thereby:

```
for (p = head; p && p->next && p->next->next; p = p->next)
    install(p);
```

Mistaking the single equal-sign assignment operator for the double equal-sign comparison operator is one of the most common C bugs. An embedded assignment in a test expression should always be tested explicitly:

```
while (*s++ = *t++)            /* BAD - resembles equality */
    ;

while ((*s++ = *t++) != '\0')   /* GOOD - avoids confusion */
    ;
```

JUSTIFICATION

The issue of bracing style is ultimately only a matter of personal opinion, but the adherants of each preference have reasons which are compelling to them. The basic position of these guidelines is that consistency within the individual project is quite an adequate level of standardization.

Most of the other rules of this section are chosen to minimize common mistakes in coding. Some aspects of consistent layout are intended to facilitate the use of automated text-handling tools.

ALTERNATIVES

Some organizations have frequent maintenance to many small projects, and prefer one organization-wide layout standard, rather than project-by-project choices.

[LOCAL NOTES]

[LOCAL NOTES]

TOPIC: 5.04 lexfns - lexical rules for functions

STANDARD

External declarations and function definitions begin at the left margin (with optional storage class and mandatory type). An explanatory comment is required before each function, and is also at the left margin. (Member functions need no comment if the functionality is obvious; see Section 4.13.) A typical one-function file looks like this:

Style #1, indented braces:

```
#include "local.h"
TYPEX varx = NNN;    // comment describing varx

// comment describing func
TYPE func(TYPE1 a1, TYPE2 a2)
    {
    <statements, including declarations>
    }
```

Style #2, exdented braces, and style #3, Kernighan & Ritchie:

```
#include "local.h"
TYPEX varx = NNN;    // comment describing varx

// comment describing func
TYPE func(TYPE1 a1, TYPE2 a2)
{
    <statements, including declarations>
}
```

In portable programs, the `main` function should be defined with no parameters, or with two parameters:

```
int main()
    {
    // ...
    }

int main(int argc, char *argv[])
    {
    // ...
    }
```

UNIX systems provide a third parameter (conventionally named `envp`) and a global pointer (named `environ`). Values in the "environment" can be changed using the `putenv` function. Neither `envp` nor `environ` nor `putenv` are portable outside UNIX or POSIX systems.

JUSTIFICATION

This layout is chosen for consistency with the layout of control structures described in Section 5.03. The essential feature here, as there, is the uniform indentation of the body and the alignment of the braces above and below the body.

ALTERNATIVES

If there is a semantic purpose for comments on the parameters of a function, format each parameter on a separate line.

Style #1, indented braces:

```
TYPE func(
    TYPE1 a1,    // comment describing a1
    TYPE2 a2)    // comment describing a2
    {
    <statements, including declarations>
    }
```

Style #2, exdented braces, and style #3, Kernighan & Ritchie:

```
TYPE func(
TYPE1 a1,    // comment describing a1
TYPE2 a2)    // comment describing a2
{
    <statements, including declarations>
}
```

[LOCAL NOTES]

TOPIC: 6.01 pragmatics - architectural issues in code re-use

GUIDELINE

Lucy Berlin [October 1990] defines *pragmatics* as "the global architecture of a component that affects *how* it provides its functionality". She describes seven dimensions in which otherwise compatible class libraries can be incompatible in practice, completely defeating the possibility of code re-use:

1.   Argument validation: The caller may expect *interactive valida-tion*, where each menu choice, or data field, or mouse click, or whatever, is validated as soon as it is chosen. But the callee may be programmed only for *declarative validation*, where all the arguments of the invoked method are checked simultaneously upon method invocation. The former is generally considered a better human-computer interaction; the latter is much easier to program.

2.   Error handling: The caller may expect errors to be reported by return values, with the caller taking responsibility for handling of errors. The callee may handle errors by non-local jump (`longjmp` in C, `throw` in C++), assuming that a higher-level handler will catch and process errors.

3.   Creation of objects: The caller may be programmed for the *outside-in* style of object creation, which provides a method for creating a new object according to specified arguments. (For example, "create a window of size x and color y".) The callee may be programmed for the *inside-out* style, in which components are interactively created first and then the composite is built from them. (For example, "Specify size. Specify color. Now create a window of that size and color.")

4.   Event-handling style: The caller may expect to have responsibility for handling asynchronous events (mouse, keyboard, etc.). The callee may expect to have the same responsibility.

5.   Responsibility for event loop: Two different subsystems may each expect to be the caller, with neither programmed to be the callee. Many User Interface Management Systems (UIMSes) expect to be the caller, while many existing applications also expect to be the caller.

6. Responsibility for cleanup: The caller may assume that the callee will perform cleanup in certain circumstances. The callee may assume that the caller will know when cleanup is needed.

7. Group operations or element operations: If group operations (e.g. "delete this list of items") are implemented as a sequence of individual operations, encapsulation purity is preserved but sometimes at great cost of efficiency (e.g. locking and unlocking databases, flushing buffers, re-indexing). On the other hand, designing in advance every possible group operation complicates the design, and many of the group operations may never be used.

It is not easy to propose a simple universal guideline to avoid these problems. Certain practices will enhance the chances for integration:

1. Argument validation: If the callee class provides validation routines for each individual argument as well as for the full list of arguments, the caller can determine which strategy best fits the problem.

2. Error handling: It is important to provide organization-wide guidelines for the uniform handling of errors. See Section 6.02 for our suggestions.

3. Creation of objects: Lucy Berlin reports "A hybrid control style (of bottom-up hints and top-down control) is possible, and we wound up using that for creation. However, such bi-directional information flow requires even tighter coupling between subsystems; it required redesign of both layers."

4. Event-handling style: Berlin reports: "In general, a philosophy that the enclosing object is in charge of its components leads to a style of object creation and event creation which makes it simple to specify common behaviors and attributes. However, it is more difficult to describe composite objects whose attributes (shape, behavior) are dynamically calculated from their contents. Each style is appropriate in different contexts, but they do not combine easily."

5. Responsibility for event loop: If a UIMS wants to be the top of the hierarchy, there is little that can be done to restructure it. However, the most flexible design for class libraries (either made or bought) is to provide methods to be *callees*. If two class libraries, both of which are callees, need to be integrated, glue code is easy to provide. If they both want to be *callers*, there is no remedy.

6.   Responsibility for cleanup: Specify as part of the class library design whether the caller or callee has responsibility for each relevant form of cleanup. One simple suggestion: if a constructor performs `new`, the destructor should perform the matching `delete` (or document why not).

7.   Group operations or element operations: At first, implement only those group operations which are known by timing estimates to be critical to system performance. (See Section 6.05.) Provide other group operations when profiling reveals hot spots.

JUSTIFICATION

It is a shame for months and years of work to go into class libraries which cannot be used with each other because of architectural differences. Planning in advance can save much effort later.

[LOCAL NOTES]

[LOCAL NOTES]

TOPIC: 6.02 errors - error-handling

GUIDELINE

There are two issues in this error-handling guideline: One is a design issue, and one is a C++ standard issue. The difficulty is that the two interact in a very tightly coupled way.

First, the design issue. Here are some alternative designs:

1. Boolean return values: The function accomplishes its operations using its arguments and uses its return value only for a status return. The trivial case is a categorization function such as `isalpha`, which returns a proper Boolean result. A more complicated example is `remove`, which returns zero for success and non-zero for failure. (Consistency would suggest that all success/fail returns should be proper Booleans, but we are all saddled with history.)

2. Augmented return values: The function produces a range of normal data return values, augmented with special values to indicate one or more categories of exceptions. A famous example is `getchar` which produces either a character value or `EOF`. IEEE floating point arithmetic uses an augmentation of normal floating-point values with special values for "positive infinity", "negative infinity", 'not-a-number', etc. Another example is the `fopen` function, which returns either a file pointer or a null pointer.

3. Inquiry functions: The exception status of prior function calls can be queried by a special function. For example, `feof` reveals the EOF status of a stream, and `ferror` reveals the error status, and `clearerr` resets both indicators. A more elaborate example might provide a "notify" function, which a function calls in order to make the error condition known to subsequent inquiry functions.

4. Terminating exceptions: E&S (1990) describes a syntax for exception-handling in C++, which has been adopted by X3J16 (although minor modifications might yet be made). Exceptions provide greater simplicity for the "normal-case" code flow: return from a called function indicates that no exceptions occurred. Occurrence of exceptions "unravels the stack" and control transfers to a `catch` clause.

This will suffice for a quick design summary. The language-standards issue is that terminating exceptions are too new to be implemented in currently-available compilers. When they are, there will then be a period of several years during which some environments will have them and some do not. But applications, and the class libraries that support them, need some guidance as to how to proceed during these years when some systems have exceptions and some don't.

Boolean return values and augmented return values are usable whether or not exceptions are implemented. If they are the simplest solution, use them.

During the transitional time, each project should define "notify" functions, per-class and system-wide, which, in an exception-handling environment, could throw a terminating exception. The project should also define the appropriate inquiry functions and reset functions. (In particular, any remaining uses of errno should always be buried inside some notify-inquiry-reset class or function.) After calling a function that could throw an exception, transitional code must assume that control *might not* have returned, but then again it might have returned even in an exceptional situation. The calling function must test the situation with inquiry functions, as frequently as is needed to avoid making invalid computations in exceptional states.

When the environment starts to support exceptions, the invocations of notify functions can be left as-is; only the implementation changes. Each occurrence of a reset is likely to become the start of a try block. The inquiry functions become harmless redundancies.

Public member functions should perform sanely even if called functions encountered errors. (This can be relaxed some day in the future, when applications routinely make use of universally-available terminating exceptions.)

JUSTIFICATION

C and C++ are pragmatic languages, used by a wide variety of projects, whose programmers take responsibility for suiting the tool to the task. It is an over-simplification to suggest one universal method.

There are a variety of design reasons to suggest providing "notify" functions, even for errors that do not alter the flow of control. The treatment of an error should be intelligently designed in view of its entire dynamic context. For example, language translators which issue dozens of identical error messages for repetitive errors could have been better designed to tabulate and summarize when some threshold is reached.

Intelligently-designed augmented return values can simplify algorithms considerably. Compare the simplicity of

```
while (iswhite(c = getchar()))
    ;
```

with the two-stage complexity of

```
while ((c = getchar()) != EOF && iswhite(c))
    ;
```

(Of course, some day many people will prefer the terminating exception.)

REFERENCES

"Clearly, there are many cases where the complexity of checking error values is manageable. In those cases, returning error values is the ideal technique." [Koenig and Stroustrup, "Exception Handling for C++", *Journal of Object-Oriented Programming*, 1990 Jul/Aug]

[LOCAL NOTES]

[LOCAL NOTES]

TOPIC: 6.03 port - portability and intentional non-portability

STANDARD

Project code should be portable across different CPU architectures, and should not depend upon word size, byte ordering, or other CPU features.

Project code should make use of only those environmental features that have been determined, during project design, to be supportable upon the range of intended project target environments.

When a module requires exceptions to these rules, the non-portable construct (asm, embedded SQL, #pragma directive, vendor-specific library call, etc.) should be encapsulated into an environment-dependent portion of the implementation. In other words, attempt to preserve a separation between the portable parts of the project and the non-portable methods employed.

The encapsulation can be embodied in alternative versions of a header file, alternative versions of a class definition, and/or alternative versions of a library.

Whenever possible, project development should take place on a variety of development environments simultaneously, so that unexpected portability problems can be detected early. It is most effective if the alternative environments represent the widest variety possible given the project's constraints.

All other factors being equal, choose the method with the later binding time.

EXAMPLE

```
prefix = "/proj/dictionary/";
        // bad - wires-in specific system

#include "environ.h"
prefix = DICTIONARY_NAME;
        // not so bad - now only the header needs changing

getnam(prefix);
        // good - dependency is in small function

prefix = getenv("DICTIONARY_NAME");
        // good - postpones binding time to run-time

config_file_name = getenv("CONFIG_FILE");
// open configuration file, and read prefix from config_file ...
fgets(prefix, sizeof(prefix), config_fp);
        // good - uses run-time binding, with only one
        // name to clutter the environment-name space
```

[LOCAL NOTES]

JUSTIFICATION

The richness of modern environmental interfaces makes the goal of strictly portable applications unrealistic in most application areas. However, the non-portable features should be logically segregated so that future porting work can be less expensive. And these guidelines attempt to prevent needless non-portability, where the environment restriction occurred simply because no one noticed it was there.

[LOCAL NOTES]

TOPIC: 6.04 measure - measuring productivity of code re-use

GUIDELINE

Everyone says that "lines of code per day" is totally obsolete as a measure of programmer productivity, but the industry has no mutually-agreed replacement for this measure. Since one of the major aims of Object-Oriented Programming is to encourage re-use, it is important to develop new management guidelines that reflect the new thinking.

To be sure, code re-use has been part of the software business for decades, in the form of third-party packages and libraries. In evaluating the "make or buy" decision, some of the important factors are functional adequacy, license restrictions, availability of support, amount and nature of royalties, memory requirements, time efficiency, and ease of programmer use.

It may be that the fundamental issue in achieving code re-use is to specify the programmer's task as the completion of functional goals, rather than the production of specified quantities of anything (lines of code, modules complete, etc.). A rational management recognizes that a programmer who spends a week researching available libraries, and finds an acceptable solution that way, has benefited the project more than a programmer who spends a week re-inventing the wheel.

A closely-related issue is progress estimation — answering the question "When will we be ready to release?". One interesting metric that has been suggested is, per week, how many changes were made to interfaces.

Another approach to structuring re-use is to create a tools group (at corporate, or divisional, and/or per-project level), with a different management, measurement, and reward structure. The tools group functions as a semi-entrepreneurial enterprise within the larger unit. They are responsible to determine the need for re-usable tools, to provide those tools, "market" those tools within the unit, and to support and maintain the tools. An internal "charge-back" system could be used in determining the cost-effectiveness of their work.

[LOCAL NOTES]

[LOCAL NOTES]

TOPIC: 6.05 effic - efficiency

STANDARD

Programs should avoid unnecessary overhead. This does not require slavish dedication to "efficiency above all else".

In Level-3 (Full C++) programs, possible sources of unnecessary overhead can come from over-generality. Many of the techniques that enhance flexibility and late binding have a negative impact upon efficiency. Intelligent engineering tradeoffs are always in order.

In Level-2 (Object-Based C++) programs, unanticipated overhead may arise from constructors in inner loops. If it is functionally necessary to declare a class variable inside a loop, indicate the reason with a comment. In this situation, the maintaining programmer will be aware of the overhead. But constructors can be invoked in circumstances not always obvious to the programmer. User requests might create a demand for vendors to provide tools to disclose non-obvious overhead (perhaps by a category of warning messages).

When possible, avoid simple arrays of constructed objects; make a class that contains the entire array. That way, its constructor can initialize the array efficiently. An "array" class also provides opportunities for bounds-checking, special I/O formatting, etc.

Avoid unnecessary temporaries. (See Section 2.01.)

Avoiding over-use of overloaded operators can help in reducing the number of temporaries. (See Section 2.02.)

When a function receives an argument of class type, use a reference parameter in preference to passing the object itself. Use a reference-to-const parameter if the function does not modify the argument. (See Section 1.06.)

Use initialization in preference to assignment. This saves one constructor and one assignment. This rule implies that declarations should appear close to the point of their usage. (See Section 1.12.)

In Level-1 (Typesafe C) programs, possible sources of unanticipated overhead may arise in the copying of aggregates:

> Initializing aggregates in automatic storage follows the "pad with zeroes" rules just as does initialization in static storage.

```
typedef struct Big { char buf[1000]; } Big;
/* ... */
for (i = 0; i < N; ++i)
    {
    Big hog = {0};   /* BAD - probably unnecessary overhead */
    /* ... */
    }
```

Passing structure arguments and returning structure results should be avoided if the structure is large. ("Large" is environment-dependent. A pair of double's, such as a complex number or a two-dimensional point, is typically considered "small". The thousand-byte structure shown above is typically considered "large".)

```
Big func(Big arg);      /* BAD - unnecessary overhead */

void func2(Big *result, Big *arg);
                        /* OK - less overhead */

bool func3(Big *result, Big *arg);
                        /* OK - return value used for success/fail */
```

JUSTIFICATION

"Abstraction" and "freedom to change the representation" do not mean that client programs can afford to absorb greatly degraded performance.

Minor syntactic convenience is not justification for diminished system performance.

GUIDELINE

In "Efficient C", Plum and Brodie discuss a development methodology which integrates efficiency concerns into the design and implementation cycle.

Item 1: Programmers and designers need to acquire an intuitive grasp of the performance characteristics of their intended targets. The simplest universal measurements are the CPU time required for the average C/C++ operations (see Section 8.02):

1. Average int operator time (for register int data);

2. Average short operator time (for auto short data);

3. Average long operator time (for auto long data);

201

4.   Average double operator time (for auto double data);

5.   Average function-call-and-return time;

6.   Average call-and-return time for a virtual function whose type is known at compile time;

7.   Average call-and-return time for a virtual function whose type is unknown at compile time.

Each application should develop its own list of basic characteristic CPU time costs (per database access, per packet transfer, per process invocation, etc).

Item 2: Designers and programmers should perform "back-of-the-envelope" estimates of the time requirements of alternative algorithms before committing major programming resources to the implementation of those algorithms. For example: "This algorithm takes 200 operators per input character. Our target machines execute 2 million operators per second, so our rough estimate of throughput is 10 thousand characters per second. This is acceptable performance, so we'll proceed to code."

Item 3: Empirical measurement ("profiling") should be used after initial implementation to determine "hot spots" (areas which account for disproportionate execution time). This information should be used in any further revisions, but only if measured performance is short of requirements. (That is, if it's fast enough, don't fine-tune it.)

If the project is following this Plum/Brodie efficiency methodology, the documentation of each function (including class members and friends) should contain information as to the average operator-count for an invocation of that member, parameterized in the most intuitive way for the application in question. For example, a polar-coordinate implementation of complex numbers may document that operator* takes six double operators. When the class-library provider proposes a changed implementation, the resulting changes in timing estimates need to be provided to clients.

[LOCAL NOTES]

[LOCAL NOTES]

TOPIC: 6.06 virtual_fct - virtual functions

GUIDELINE

Projects with a commitment to object-oriented techniques should use derived classes and virtual functions. Using virtual functions is the key distinction between programming in Full C++ vs. programming in Òbject-Based C++ (see Section 0.02, levels of use).

Virtual functions enable a client to manipulate objects of different (derived) classes through a common interface defined by the base. Through virtual functions, an object exhibits the behavior of the derived class by which it was declared, not the base class by which it is referenced. Virtual functions simplify interfaces between classes and clients and improve system maintainability.

However, not every function in a base class needs to be virtual. A function whose behavior differs among the derived classes should be virtual. A function whose behavior is the same among the derived classes should not be virtual. When execution speed is critical, a frequently called function should not be virtual. Gorlen, et. al. (1990) caution against declaring a virtual function as inline. Depending on the compiler, it may increase the code size without improving execution speed.

A class that is not intended to serve as a base class should have no virtual functions.

When using object-oriented methods and Full C++, use derived classes with virtual functions rather than discriminated unions and switch statements to distinguish the behavior of subclasses. A *discriminated union* is a union with an associated type field. The type field selects an alternative member of the union.

Also, when programming in Full C++, avoid enumerating the classes in a hierarchy of derived classes. That is, do not declare an enumeration type with one enumerator for each class in a derivation hierarchy. Do not declare arrays such that each element in the array corresponds to one class in the hierarchy.

EXAMPLE

A *shape* is a planar geometric object, such as *circle*, *rectangle*, and *triangle*, with properties such as *name, area* and *perimeter*. Using discriminated unions when programming in Typesafe C, the implementation of shapes looks like:

```
enum shape_code {CIRCLE, RECTANGLE, TRIANGLE};
        // one enumerator for each shape
const char *shape_name[] = {"circle", "rectangle", "triangle"};
        // one array element for each shape

struct circle
    {
    double radius;
    };
struct rectangle
    {
    double height, width;
    };
struct triangle
    {
    double side1, side2, angle;
    };
struct shape
    {
    shape_code sc;        // type field
    union                 // discriminated union
        {
        circle c;
        rectangle r;
        triangle t;
        };
    };

double area(shape &s)
    {
    switch (s.sc)         // one case for each shape
        {
    case CIRCLE:
        return PI * s.c.radius * s.c.radius;
    case RECTANGLE:
        return s.r.height * s.r.width;
    case TRIANGLE:
        return s.t.side1 * sin(s.t.angle) * s.t.side2 / 2;
    default:
        // error ...
        };
    };

double perimeter(shape &s)
    {
    switch (s.sc)
        // one case for each shape...
    };
```

Using derived classes and virtual functions in Full C++, the same example looks like:

```
class shape
    {
public:
    virtual double area() const = 0;
    virtual double perimeter() const = 0;
        // OK - uses virtual function instead of union
    virtual const char *name() const = 0;
        // OK - uses virtual function instead of array of names
    };

class circle : public shape
    {
public:
    circle(double r = 0) : radius(r) { }
    double area() const { return pi * radius * radius; }
    double perimeter() const { // ... }
    const char *name() const { return "circle"; }
private:
    double radius;
    };

class rectangle : public shape
    {
public:
    rectangle(double h = 0, double w = 0)
        : height(h), width(w) { }
    double area() const { return height * width; }
    double perimeter() const { // ... }
    const char *name() const { return "rectangle"; }
private:
    double height, width;
    };

class triangle : public shape
    {
public:
    triangle(double s1 = 0, double s2 = 0, double a = 0)
        : side1(s1), side2(s2), angle(a) { }
    double area() const
        { return side1 * sin(angle) * side2 / 2; };
    double perimeter() const { // ... };
    const char *name() const { return "triangle"; }
private:
    double side1, side2, angle;
    };
```

JUSTIFICATION

Virtual functions are more powerful and flexible than non-virtual functions. Russo and Kaplan (1988) have demonstrated that thoughtful use of virtual functions can actually improve a program's overall execution speed.

However, each virtual function call usually generates more code and executes slower than a non-virtual call. Gorlen, et. al. (1990) found that the invocation overhead of a virtual function call is roughly twice that of a non-virtual call. Thus, routinely declaring all functions in a base class as virtual may degrade program performance unnecessarily.

Using derived classes and virtual functions is more flexible and maintainable than using discriminated unions and switch statements. To add another shape using derived classes, simply derive another class from shape, say ellipse, and redefine the virtual functions area, name and perimeter for that shape. Only those source files that specifically manipulate ellipse objects need to be recompiled. Files that manipulate shapes need not be recompiled.

To add ellipses using discriminated unions, many changes must be made. You must add ELLIPSE as a new enumerator in shape_code and create a new struct ellipse. You must add a new case to the switch statements in every function like area and perimeter. Also, you must add "ellipse" as another element in the shape_name array.

ALTERNATIVES

Using a type code for each class in a derivation hierarchy may be unavoidable at the point in a program that actually creates objects. For example, a menu system that creates geometric objects needs to know how many different objects there are so it can present the choices. When the user makes a choice, the program must translate that choice into a call on a constructor for the selected shape.

[LOCAL NOTES]

207

TOPIC: 6.07 virtual_dtor - virtual destructors

GUIDELINE

A base class B should have a virtual destructor whenever all of the following conditions hold:

1.   B has at least one derived class D.

2.   D's destructor is different from B's destructor.

3.   a D objects might be deleted via a pointer or reference to a B.

D's destructor would be different from B's destructor if D objects managed the B sub-object differently, or if D's class definition had additional data members with their own destructors.

A class that is not intended for use as a base class need not have a virtual destructor. By definition, classes written in Object-Based C++ do not have virtual destructors.

There is one case in which a virtual destructor doesn't help: an array of derived class objects cannot be deleted via a pointer to the base class, because the translator cannot determine the actual size of the array elements. The element size is needed to calculate the `this` pointers passed to the destructor of each element.

JUSTIFICATION

Consider the behavior of the following example:

```
class Vector
    {
    // ...
public:
    // ...
    ~Vector();
    };

class B
    {
    char *p;
public:
    B(size_t n) { p = new char[n]; }
    ~B() { delete p; }
    // ...
    };
```

[LOCAL NOTES]

TOPIC: 6.09 protected - protected members

GUIDELINE

Internal functions (used only by members and friends) of a class should be member functions. Internal functions intended for use by derived classes should be protected members. All other internal functions should be private.

Avoid public and protected data members in a base class for an abstract data type (Section 1.01). (The members of just-a-struct are always public. See Section 1.02.) If, for efficiency reasons, a derived class needs special access to the representation of its base class, provide the base with protected inline accessor and mutator functions instead of protected data members.

Use private derivation to make inherited protected members inaccessible to further derived classes. Use public derivation to propagate protected members downward through a class hierarchy.

JUSTIFICATION

Good software design reduces coupling between components. Private access completely prevents coupling. Protected access only allows coupling between a base class and its derived classes. Public access enables coupling. Well-designed classes do not eliminate coupling. However, they minimize coupling by favoring the most restrictive access control possible.

Inheritance is by its nature a tight logical coupling between a base and its derived classes. However, that coupling need not be a tight physical coupling. Protected data members couple a base class to its derived classes, just as public data members couple a class to its clients. Inline accessors and mutators loosen that coupling with no loss of efficiency.

[LOCAL NOTES]

[LOCAL NOTES]

TOPIC: 6.10 firewalls - compilation firewalls

GUIDELINE

The private members of a class definition are inaccessible to client code, so changes in the private members don't cause changes in the client's source code. However, when the entire class definition appears in a class header, changes in the private members force recompilation when make tools depend only upon file version dates. In large class hierarchies and applications, this recompilation can be time-consuming and burdensome. Such projects should employ the following techniques to minimize such recompilation, by creating "compilation firewalls" (Booch, 1991).

Carolan (1991) recommends the "Cheshire Cat" technique: move the private data for a class into a separate class (an "implementation" class) in a separate header, and access the implementation class via a single private pointer in the original class.

For example, suppose a class for a menu system looks like

```
// Menu.h

class Menu
    {
    int no_entries;
    // ...
public:
    Menu(int entries) : no_entries(entries) { }
    // ...
    };
```

Adding a new private data member, say pixel_width, doesn't change the public and protected interfaces, but causes a recompilation of any source file that includes Menu.h. Using the Cheshire Cat technique, move Menu's private data to a new implementation class MenuImp, as follows

```
// MenuImp.h

class Menu;

class MenuImp
    {
    friend class Menu;
    int no_entries;
    int pixel_width;
    // ...
    };
```

and rewrite Menu.h as

```
// Menu.h
class MenuImp;

class Menu
    {
    MenuImp *p;
public:
    Menu(int entries);
    // ...
    };
```

Borrowing terminology from the C standard, declaring only the name of class MenuImp makes it an *incomplete type*. A source file can declare pointers to incomplete types, but not dereference them. Thus, Menu's constructor can no longer be an inline function, because the details of MenuImp aren't available to source files that include Menu.h only. The constructor must defined elsewhere, as

```
Menu::Menu(int entries)
    {
    p = new MenuImp;
    p->no_entries = entries;
    }
```

The Cheshire Cat technique produces a solid compilation firewall. It also conserves stack space, by shifting private data to the free store. In return, classes applying this technique suffer a performance penalty:

1. They cannot have any inline member functions.

2. Every member function must reference the private data via a pointer.

In most cases, attempts to allocate an object of the implementation class or dereference to pointer to the implementation object will be caught by the compiler. However, many C++ translators permit

```
delete p;
```

where p is a pointer to an incomplete type. This delete deallocates the storage referenced by p, but fails to call its destructor (if any), so don't delete pointers to incomplete types.

Gorlen, et. al. (1990) suggest a technique for avoiding recompilations caused by changes in private static data members. Static data members are part of the class declaration, and therefore appear in the header file containing that declaration. If the declaration of the static data members change, every source file that includes the header must be recompiled. To avoid recompilation, use non-member static data instead of static data members when a class

1.　　is implemented in a single source module, and

2.　　has no inline functions that access the static data of the class.

Static non-member data need only appear in the source file that implements the class; it need not be in the header. If the static data ever changes, only the one source file must be recompiled.

[LOCAL NOTES]

　　　　　　　Copyright © 1991, Thomas Plum and Dan Saks

[LOCAL NOTES]

TOPIC: 6.11 comments - suggested use of comments

GUIDELINE

A function which performs a simple transformation on its arguments may adequately be documented by a one-line "verb + objects" header comment. For larger or more complicated functions, a good explanatory comment should describe the important data structures used and should depict the control flow with a few lines of "pseudo-code" or "program design language".

Ideally, the use of meaningful variable names and clear control structures will eliminate the need for line-by-line commenting, but each "paragraph" or logical grouping of statements will be made more readable by a comment prior to the block, indented at the same level as the statements.

Where an individual statement needs clarification (even after attempts to clarify the code itself), its explanatory comment is placed at the right of the line being explained. This form of comment is also useful for describing declarations.

A related guideline for other variable declarations is that a declaration which specifies an initial value will declare only one variable, and a comment can conveniently be placed at the right of the line.

Use `#if 0` if there is a need to comment-out sections of code. Comments do not nest.

JUSTIFICATION

Following the style of examples shown in programming textbooks usually gives insufficient clues about what the function does; this is because textbooks actually contain the "comments" in the text of the book.

One good practical test of the amount of commenting needed is this: "Can the reviewer understand the function without detailed coaching from the author?".

It must be recognized that there is such a thing as over-commenting, which restates the obvious and slows down comprehension by sheer weight of reading matter. Therefore, individual judgement is needed.

[LOCAL NOTES]

[LOCAL NOTES]

TOPIC: 6.12 specs - specifications

STANDARD

A program must be unmistakably matched to an external specification.

The program must meet all the demands of its specification. In other words, the program must work.

If a program consists of multiple source files, there must be a visible way to tell what files these are (since its specification applies to the entire set). One common way to show the correspondence is in the "Makefile" which shows the command which compiles the main function. For example, the command

```
cc -o mainpgm mainpgm.o file2.o file3.o
```

shows the three files involved.

JUSTIFICATION

That the program works correctly is the fundamental criterion.

Verifying its correctness requires a specification to check it against.

[LOCAL NOTES]

[LOCAL NOTES]

TOPIC: 6.13 reviews - code reviews

STANDARD

If a program is to be part of a released product, the program must be reviewed by one or more people other than its author.

The names of author and reviewer(s) must be documented in a comment.

The reviewer's concurrence means "I have read all the code and its corresponding specification. As best I can tell, the program is understandable, meets its specification, and conforms to all applicable standards. I would be able to maintain it."

Requisite efficiency may be considered a part of the specification, and should be spelled out explicitly in critical cases.

The review process applies to the entire source file, rather than to each function separately; the source file is the basic entity for software administration.

Each project whose management supports the resources for *correct, reliable code* will conduct some form of structured code reviews, such as "first-order correctness reviews":

> **First-order correctness review:** A review that produces a hard-copy list of test cases that would be needed in order to bracket all boundary values and to test all distinct cases (of both program and specification). (Testing "all distinct cases" guarantees "branch coverage" — all Boolean results are made to be *true* by some test case, and *false* by some other test case.)

The report from a first-order correctness review can conveniently be used for subsequent *first-order correctness testing*, which produces an automated regression test.

JUSTIFICATION

There is a class of bugs known as "blind spots" which will never be found by the author. This means that all applications that require *correctness* in the product must have some procedure for review by someone other than the author.

It is desirable to have a procedure such as "code review" or "walk-through" which formalizes the review process, but even without formal processes, the interests of future maintainers demand that the program must be understandable by someone other than its original author.

       Copyright © 1991, Thomas Plum and Dan Saks

For more details about first-order testing, refer to Section 8.01 in this manual.

[LOCAL NOTES]

TOPIC: 6.14 defensive - defensive programming

STANDARD

Programs should not "blow up" or behave unpredictably in the face of out-of-bounds data (including I/O problems like "out of space"). This does not mean that programs are required to explicitly *diagnose* every out-of-bounds condition — only that they should behave sensibly. Nor does it mean that every function is required to perform bounds-checking. For non-member functions, the requirement is that some-where within each source file must be found the code that will protect against out-of-bounds data. For class member functions, each public member function is responsible to protect the client against out-of-bounds data.

Regarding the I/O library functions, two methods are acceptable:

1. Check every returned value from each function which provides error information. (Simply casting the function call to (void) is worse than nothing in this regard, and is to be avoided.)

2. Test the error status of each file, using ferror, as often as desired. Before closing the file, flush its last buffer before the final ferror test:

```
/* all finished with file fp */
fflush(fp);
if (ferror(fp))
    /* handle the error situation */
fclose(fp);
```

3. When all your environments support terminating exceptions, design all I/O access so that exceptions are thrown when any I/O error takes place. (See Section 6.02.)

JUSTIFICATION

Specifications should not be burdened with case-by-case requirements that programs behave sensibly; this should be assumed as a quality of professional software.

On the other hand, requiring bounds-checking on every statement or even every function can be grossly inefficient.

As described in Section 0.01, exceptions must be noted in comments.

[LOCAL NOTES]

[LOCAL NOTES]

TOPIC: 6.15 simplicity - simplicity of design and implementation

GUIDELINE

Keep it simple.

Needless complexity contributes to unreliability.

Estimate in advance the necessary areas of generality, then meet them. Do not generalize everything.

Estimate in advance the likely future requirements of portability, then meet them. Do not attempt portability to any and all conceivable future environments, unless that is an agreed-upon requirement of the project.

[LOCAL NOTES]

[LOCAL NOTES]

TOPIC: 7.01 versions – versions of C++

GUIDELINE

Portable programs should avoid anachronistic features:

1.   Avoid the keyword `overload`.

2.   Always initialize static data members explicitly.

3.   Do not assign an `int` to an object of enumeration type.

4.   Always invoke the niladic `operator++()` and `operator--()` using prefix notation, i.e., `++x` and not `x++`.

5.   Do not use old-style C function definitions.

6.   Do not omit the base class name from the initializer list of a derived class constructor:

```
class B
  {
public:
  B(int);
  };

class D : public B
  {
  D(int i) : (i) { }      // BAD - anachronistic
  D(int i) : B(i) { }     // OK - uses base class name
  };
```

7.   Do not assign to `this`. Use an overloaded `new` operator with the placement syntax.

8.   Do not cast a pointer to a member function to a pointer to a function.

Avoiding these anachronisms is simple. The following complexities are not.

Until there is a widely-implemented standard for C++, portable C++ programs should use version-dependent features only when their target environments support them. The availability of the following features needs to be assessed in each target environment:

1.   Nested types (Section 1.11).

2.   Allowing a constructor with all default arguments to serve as a default constructor.

228   Copyright © 1991, Thomas Plum and Dan Saks

3. Overloading operators ++ and -- with an argument (to define postfix operators).

4. Parameterized types, using `template` classes and functions (Section 1.15 and Section 7.06).

5. Exceptions, using `try` blocks, `catch` clauses and `throw` expressions (Section 6.01).

6. Allowing a `static const` data member in a constant expression. For example,

```
class X
    {
public:
    static const int n;
    };

const int X::n = 100;

int foo()
    {
    int a[X::n];    // not allowed in older versions
    // ...
    }
```

7. Use of the `volatile` qualifier.

8. Differences between the Release 2.0 and 2.1 versions of `delete` for arrays. (The 2.0 form will probably be supported for some time to come.)

```
delete [N] p;   // 2.0 version
delete [] p;    // 2.1 version
```

JUSTIFICATION

The ANSI technical committee X3J16 is currently developing a standard for C++; however they are not likely to complete the standard until 1992 at least. The emerging standard is based primarily on The AT&T C++ Language System Release 2.1 Product Reference Manual (an annotated version appears in E&S (1990)), and secondarily on the ANSI C Standard (X3.159-1989). However, no implementations of the language described by E&S are commercially available as of this writing. Although there is little doubt that the eventual standard will be very similar to E&S (1990), programmers naturally cannot use those features that are not available in their current C++ translators.

Some features of early C++ translators are already anachronisms. They are still supported by most C++ translators, but have been supplanted by newer and better features. Some anachronisms may not be included in the eventual C++ standard.

[LOCAL NOTES]

[LOCAL NOTES]

TOPIC: 7.02 C_problems - problem areas from C

GUIDELINE

Avoid C language features that conflict with programming in C++:

1.   Do not use `setjmp` and `longjmp` if there are any objects with destructors which could be created between the execution of the `setjmp` and the `longjmp`.

2.   Do not use the `offsetof` macro except when applied to members of just-a-struct.

3.   Do not mix C-style `FILE` I/O (using `stdio.h`) with C++ style I/O (using `iostream.h` or `stream.h`) on the same file.

4.   Avoid using C functions like `memcpy` or `memcmp` for copying or comparing objects of a type other than array-of-`char` or just-a-struct (Section 1.01).

5.   Avoid the C macro `NULL`; use 0 instead (Section 1.06).

JUSTIFICATION

Each of these features concerns an area of traditional C usage which creates some problem in C++.

[LOCAL NOTES]

[LOCAL NOTES]

TOPIC: 7.03 when - when to use C, when to use C++

GUIDELINE

The C Language has a Standard, the identically-worded documents X3.159-1989 (ANSI) and ISO/IEC 9899 (ISO, 1990). (The page numbers and major section numbers differ in the two documents.) The C++ Language is in the process of standardization. Therefore, C will (for a while) be favored by projects that lay heavy stress upon bug-free compilers, wide portability, and precise target semantics.

Projects working in C++ must expect periodic revisions of their source code to accommodate revisions in the compilers which track the draft standard. (For a project with a multi-year development horizon, this may provide little problem.)

It is, of course, worth mentioning that "C versus C++" is, in one way, a false dichotomy: all projects currently working in ANSI/ISO Standard C should follow the Guidelines in this book for programming in typesafe C, (the common subset of C and C++). (See Section 7.04.)

Having said all this, the reason Plum and Saks are collaborating on this book is that, in our opinion, most projects which are currently working in C will within, say, three years, find that C++ is the preferable language for their work. Another way of saying this opinion is that C++ appears likely to be the evolution path of most projects currently working in C. If this is true, then for these projects the question is not whether to migrate to C++, but when to migrate.

We have no hard-and-fast data yet. Some commentators suggest that *any* new large project (e.g. one that expects 100K lines of code) should make use of C++ for the greater software-management control that it provides.

Application areas already known to be object-oriented are appropriate areas for the immediate switch to C++.

Each technical area should be sponsoring pilot projects now, investigating the suitability of C++ for that area's work. When success with the pilot projects indicates the suitability of C++ for that application area, subsequent projects should consider the relevant advantages of C++.

[LOCAL NOTES]

[LOCAL NOTES]

TOPIC: 7.04 TypesafeC - the intersection of Standard C and C++

STANDARD

There are two situations in which projects should work in *Typesafe C*, the common subset of Standard C and C++:

1.   Where the project is developing source code for some environments which have C++, and also for other environments which have only C.

2.   Where the current environment supports C but not C++, but the project anticipates migration to C++.

In either case, general-purpose functions which are applicable to both C and C++ environments should be written in Typesafe C.

Operationally, such functions should be compiled and tested on both a Standard C environment and a C++ environment. This way, the dozens of specific syntactic restrictions will be enforced automatically by the compilers and do not need to be restated here.

The following guidelines summarize, for C programmers, the techniques of writing in Typesafe C.

Avoid the new keywords of C++:

```
asm  catch  class  delete  friend  inline  new  operator
private  protected  public  template  this  throw  try  virtual
```

Certain other words have been tentatively proposed as new keywords; cautious programmers would avoid them:

```
and  or  bitand  bitor  bitxor  bitcompl
```

Do not use double-underscore in any identifier (except for those in Standard macro names such as `__LINE__` etc.)

Confine your use of the `sizeof` operator to lvalue expressions (such as the name of a variable) or to type names. Avoid applying `sizeof` to rvalue expressions:

```
n = sizeof(buf);        /* OK - size of a variable */
n = sizeof(struct s);   /* OK - size of a type */
n = sizeof('a');        /* BAD - size of an rvalue, C and C++ differ */
```

Each tag name should be explicitly `typedef`'ed to be its own synonym:

```
typedef struct symbol symbol;
```

The equivalence is established automatically by C++.

All file-scope const data should have explicit storage-class (static or extern). (There will be many fewer file-scope const's in Typesafe C than in C++, because C does not recognize them in constant expressions; therefore, enumerators or #define'd macro constants are needed in Typesafe C.)

Treat each enumeration as a distinct type. (However, you can safely assume that enumerators promote to integers.)

C++ will insist upon the function prototype syntax for all definitions and declarations of functions. Use it everywhere, preferably in header files.

Regarding niladic functions (those that take no arguments): when defining niladic functions, use empty parentheses:

```
int f() { /* ... */ }  // OK - definition uses empty parentheses
```

How to declare niladic function prototypes depends upon the future uses of the Typesafe C source code. If the headers will be shipped to C-only projects (which will depend upon the prototype-checking of the C compiler), use f(void) in prototypes:

```
int f(void);          // OK - C-only projects get argument-checking
```

If the headers will only be used on projects that will routinely compile with the C++ compiler (which treats f() as equivalent to f(void)), then use f() in prototypes:

```
int f();              // OK - C++ projects get argument-checking
```

And if you don't know where the headers will be used, be conservative with f(void).

When programming in Typesafe C, you should usually not use extern "C". The Typesafe C source files should either (a) be compiled as C++ to produce C++ object code, for a project that uses C++, or (b) be compiled as C to produce C object code, for a project using only C. In either case, the native linkage is used.

The only exception to this avoidance of extern "C" is when Typesafe C is compiled into an object library which is supposed to be linkable either from C or from C++ in the same executable program. Then, the headers supplied with the library should bracket all the function declarations with

```
#ifdef __cplusplus
extern "C" {
#endif
    /* function declarations here */
#ifdef __cplusplus
}
#endif
```

Any construct that must be expressed differently in C++ should be made conditional upon the macro __cplusplus. (But there should be no need for this in Typesafe C.)

In C++, any generic (void*) pointer value must be explicitly converted when assigning it to a non-generic pointer:

```
void *genericfn();

char *p = (char *)genericfn();
```

In C++, there is no "common linkage" (or "tentative definition");

```
int i;
int i;
```

is a syntax error.

JUSTIFICATION

If there is no functional reason why a function is confined to C only, or to C++ only, then it is a needless restriction upon code re-use to limit its use by unintentional syntactic features.

[LOCAL NOTES]

[LOCAL NOTES]

TOPIC: 7.05 mixing - mixing C and C++ code

GUIDELINE

The easiest way to mix C and C++ code is to write the C in Typesafe C and compile it as C++. (See Section 0.02.) Alternatively, use the `extern "C"` wrapper for linkage of names.

The function `main` should be a C++ function. (This is the simplest way to be sure that static initializers are handled properly.)

Avoid the C constructs that create problems in C++ (Section 7.02).

Interrupt handlers, if written in C for establishment via `signal`, should simply set a `sig_atomic_t` flag somewhere and return. The main program flow should inquire about such flags when needed. (This is a special case of the notify/inquire pattern described in Section 6.01.) In some environments, the interrupt handlers may need to be established in a manner different from the ANSI C signal function.

JUSTIFICATION

The degree to which C++ libraries must provide expected semantics for the Standard C library is still under debate by X3J16. These guidelines are a condensation of current likelihoods.

REFERENCES

Steve Clamage, "ANSI C Library Compatibility Issues", X3J16/90-0105, November 13, 1990.

Jerry Schwarz, "Mixed C and C++ Environments", X3J16/91-0011, February 8, 1991.

[LOCAL NOTES]

[LOCAL NOTES]

TOPIC: 7.06 paramtypes - parameterized types

GUIDELINE

Use template classes (Section 1.15). If templates are unavailable, simulate parameterized types using a mechanism that preserves static typing, or avoid parameterized types altogether. Do not use polymorphism (derived class with virtual functions) or void * to simulate parameterized types (Section 1.15).

If templates are unavailable, projects should adopt one of the following policies toward parameterized types:

1. Use the preprocessor macros defined in <generic.h> to implement parameterized types. The technique is demonstrated in Stroustrup (1986).

2. Use an enhanced macro processor that recognizes a close approximation to the template syntax in E&S (1990), such as Texas Instruments COOL preprocessor described by Fontana, et. al. (1990). A project should use unsupported preprocessing tools only if that project will support the tools itself.

3. Use no parameterized types. Implement all classes using specific component types.

JUSTIFICATION

C++ is a statically typed language. That is, it determines at translation-time whether an operation can be applied to a particular set of operands. Not only does static typing improve program reliability, it enables C++ translators to generate code which is competitive with C.

Template classes and functions provide an efficient, typesafe way to define reusable container classes. Template expansion occurs at translation time and preserves the static typing of C++. Any simulation of parameterized types should also preserve static typing. Macros and specialized preprocessors do just that.

Using polymorphism to simulate parameterized types is an attempt to defeat the static type checking by deriving all objects from a common object. Containers of polymorphic objects are "heterogeneous"; without run-time checking, they cannot prevent inadvertent mixing of different types of objects in a single container (Section 1.15). Containers of void * are containers of typeless objects. They are unsafe and should be avoided.

242   Copyright © 1991, Thomas Plum and Dan Saks

[LOCAL NOTES]

TOPIC:　　8.01 review - first-order correctness review and test

The programming field could use a "generally accepted" criterion for a reasonable amount of review and testing. It is time to bring some over-simplification to an overly-complicated problem.

What we need is a procedure which could be taught in one session of any programming course, to serve as a reasonable minimum upon program verification. Too often, we now teach programming like a driver-instruction course that omits mention of brakes.

Each particular development standard requires different deliverables, but they all include source code (at least). The proposal described here is that the source code should be accompanied by a specific set of review notes. If testing is part of the programmer's job, a specific criterion for testing should also be followed.

The procedures are called *first-order correctness review* and *first-order correctness test*.

WHAT IS A FIRST-ORDER CORRECTNESS REVIEW AND TEST

Here are two criteria adapted from Glen Myers' *Art of Software Testing*:

Boundary values (limits upon program performance): Each valid boundary value should be tested, and the adjacent invalid value should also be tested.

Distinct cases (or "equivalence classes"): Each distinct behavior of the program should be exercised by one representative test case.

From the original specification, different input cases, different output cases, and different internal states all suggest distinct cases to be tested. From the program source listing, further distinct cases can be systematically listed by considering what data values are required to make each individual conditional to be *TRUE* in one case and *FALSE* in some other case. (This means that tests for "all distinct cases" are a superset of the tests for "branch coverage", which forces every potential branch to be executed.)

A *first-order test*, then, is one which meets these criteria.

A *first-order review* is one which produces an on-paper list of the cases which would be needed for a first-order test. The agenda for the code review is the actual production of this list.

Besides testable cases, the review should identify "untestable" exception cases. In a reliable program, each exception case is prevented from happening by some guarantee elsewhere in the program, or in the documentation, the specification, or the language standard. The review should document each such guarantee.

The exception cases can be indicated by abbreviations such as this:

ABBREV	OPERATORS			DESCRIPTION OF EXCEPTION CASES
OOB	a[n]	a<<n	a>>n	"Out Of Bounds" subscript or shift count
BAD_P	*p	p[n]	p->m	"Bad pointer" -- out-of-bounds, dangling, or null pointer
OFLO	a*b ++a --a	a+b a++ a--	a-b	"Overflow" -- a signed-arithmetic or pointer expression overflow
UFLO	a*b a+b	a/b a-b		"Underflow" -- a floating-point expression result too small to represent
CHOP	a=b	f(a)		"Chop" or "Truncation" -- assignment, or calling prototyped-function, that loses bits
DIV_0	a/b	a%b		"Divide-by-zero"
XALIGN	(ptr *)			"Mis-alignment" -- a pointer cast that loses alignment information

A similar table should be produced for each library of called functions used by the application, and used in the review of exceptions and distinct cases. (The simple example below calls no library functions.)

These review and test procedures are called "first-order" because there is no attempt to deal with the (combinatorially-large) set of interactions between individual conditionals; each one is analyzed independently.

HOW TO DO A FIRST-ORDER REVIEW

Let us examine a specific little example, and show what a first-order review would produce. Consider a portable C implementation of the Standard Library function strcmp, which is now required to use unsigned char logic in comparisons:

```
1    /* strcmp - compare (unsigned) strings  */
2    int strcmp(
3        register const char s[],   /* : string */
4        register const char t[])   /* : string */
5        {
6        typedef unsigned char uchar;
7
8        while (*s != '\0' && *s == *t)
9            {
10           ++s;
11           ++t;
12           }
13       if (*(uchar *)s < *(uchar *)t)
14           return -1;
15       else if (*(uchar *)s == *(uchar *)t)
16           return 0;
17       else
18           return 1;
19       }
```

The review proceeds through the program line-by-line, identifying distinct cases, boundary values, and assumptions on each line.

On line 8, the logical-and condition has three possible outcomes: *FALSE* immediately, *TRUE* on the left and *FALSE* on the right, and both sides *TRUE*. The only possible exception is *BAD_P* ("bad pointer").

On lines 10 and 11, an *OFLO* is possible ("pointer wrap-around").

Line 13 has two testable outcomes (FALSE and *TRUE*). The pointer cast has a potential *XALIGN*.

On line 14 (the outcome when string s compares low to string t), the minimum boundary value for *s (considered as an unsigned char) is zero; the maximum boundary value for *t is UCHAR_MAX. There are no invalid values to test.

Line 15 has two Boolean outcomes, and no new exceptions.

Line 18 would be reached by a boundary case that matches the maximum *s with the minimum *t.

So far, the review notes look like this:


```
LIST OF TEST CASES    PROGRAM LISTING                        EXCEPTIONS?
.................     ....................................   ...........
__F  __TF  __TT   8   while (*s != '\0' && *s == *t)         ___BAD_P
                  9   {
                 10     ++s;                                  ___OFLO
                 11     ++t;                                  ___OFLO
                 12   }
__F      __T     13   if (*(uchar *)s < *(uchar *)t)          ___XALIGN
__MIN *s __MAX *t 14     return -1;
__F      __T     15   else if (*(uchar *)s == *(uchar *)t)
                 16     return 0;
                 17   else
__MAX *s __MIN *t 18     return 1;
```

Next, the review returns to the specification. There are three distinct cases — low, equal, high — and these are assigned test cases numbered 1, 2, and 3.

The specification indicates that s and t must point to strings (i.e., properly null-terminated). This requirement will receive an item number soon.

The review notes look like this:

```
REVIEWER'S NOTES    SPECIFICATION
.................   ...................................
                    Outcomes of returned value:
_1_                   Less than zero:     s compares low to t
_2_                   Zero:               s compares equal to t
_3_                   Greater than zero:  s compares high to t
                    Parameters  s  and  t  must point to strings,
___                   properly null-terminated.
```

Now specific test cases are chosen, attempting wherever possible to use one case to cover both a boundary-value test and a distinct-case test:

```
TEST CASES AND DESCRIPTIONS
...............................................................

1.  s is null string, t starts with largest unsigned char value
2.  s and t are equal strings, e.g.  "a"
3.  s starts with largest unsigned char value, t is null string
```

The review fills in the blanks next to each boundary-value and distinct-case test. In this example, the three cases chosen from the specification are sufficient to achieve both coverages.

Next, the review documents the reasons why each possible exception cannot happen:

```
GUARANTEES AGAINST EXCEPTIONS
-------------------------------------------------------------
4.  Specification: strings s and t are null-terminated,
    so the pointer increments cannot overflow.
5.  C Standard: unsigned char has the same alignment as char.
```

The annotated program listing now looks like this:

```
LIST OF TEST CASES     PROGRAM LISTING                       EXCEPTIONS?
------------------     ---------------------------------     -----------
_1_F    _3_TF  _2_TT   8   while (*s != '\0' && *s == *t)     _4_BAD_P
                       9   {
                       10      ++s;                           _4_OFLO
                       11      ++t;                           _4_OFLO
                       12   }
_3_F         _1_T      13  if (*(uchar *)s < *(uchar *)t)     _5_XALIGN
_1_MIN *s  _1_MAX *t   14     return -1;
_3_F         _2_T      15  else if (*(uchar *)s == *(uchar *)t)
                       16     return 0;
                       17  else
_3_MAX *s  _3_MIN *t   18     return 1;
```

In this simple example, the actual program to apply the first-order test coverage is simple to construct:

```
TEST PROGRAM
-------------------------------------------------------------
#include <limits.h>
#include <assert.h>
#undef NDEBUG    /* turn on assert's */
char s_max[2] = {UCHAR_MAX, '\0'};  /* string with largest uchar */
int main()
    {
    assert(strcmp("", s_max) < 0);  /* case 1 */
    assert(strcmp("a", "a") == 0);  /* case 2 */
    assert(strcmp(s_max, "") > 0);  /* case 3 */
    exit(0);
    }
```

If an automated test-coverage analyzer is available ("branch-coverage" verifier), execution of this test driver can be shown mechanically to have covered all Boolean outcomes. Even more useful would be automated assistance in static checking of the exception-preventing guarantees ("Super-lint").

WHY THIS PARTICULAR APPROACH?

This methodology is suggested for projects and situations in which correctness and reliability are of paramount importance. (As an industry we may still undervalue these qualities in practice, but we all learn from experience.)

Mathematical techniques ("correctness proofs") have been suggested for this purpose, but most application areas are not formally axiomatized. Proofs, and other commendable approaches to analysis and design, do not by themselves supply a means of verifying that the design was properly implemented. Furthermore, many embedded applications interact with hardware and interfaces whose correct behavior cannot be formally assumed. Review, and subsequent testing, close the loop of verifiability.

Some people tout high-level languages that perform run-time checking as the path to reliability in practice. But a better approach is to *prevent* run-time exceptions by properly-coded program logic, not by patching up after they have occurred.

With regard to the review agenda, discussing the program in terms of specific test cases provides a language which is understandable to all parties — users, analysts, designers, and programmers. The first-order review discusses the program using systematically chosen examples.

As a practical matter, most of the first-order reviews that we have seen in practice have produced useful results — finding errors, improving documentation, or locating ambiguities in specifications. Plum Hall would be glad to hear about the experiences that your project has with techniques like this.

[*This material first appeared as an article in* **C Users Journal**, *December/January 1989, Vol 7, No 1, Pages 75-78.*]

TOPIC: 8.02 benches – simple benchmark programs

For several years, compiler evaluators have used the Plum Hall low-level benchmark programs to measure fundamental CPU-time usage of the code generated by C compilers. These benchmarks produce "average operator" time measurements that are useful in "back-of-the-envelope" efficiency estimating.

Here we present a revised version of the C benchmark (named bench2.c), and a new benchmark for C++ (named bench3.c).

The bench2.c program, written in Typesafe C, produces a table of execution times, in microseconds, for five basic CPU-time factors of C (or C++) programs:

1.   Average int operator time (for register int data);

2.   Average short operator time (for auto short data);

3.   Average long operator time (for auto long data);

4.   Average double operator time (for auto double data);

5.   Average function-call-and-return time.

The bench3.c program, written in C++, produces two more execution times in microseconds:

6.   Average call-and-return time for a virtual function whose type is known at compile time;

7.   Average call-and-return time for a virtual function whose type is unknown at compile time;

Each benchmark is designed to produce results that truly depend functionally upon a command-line argument inaccessible to the compiler, so that code is not "optimized away". (There is always the possibility, of course, that a vendor will introduce a "Plum-Hall-benchmark-recognizer" feature to enhance product publicity.)

The numbers obtained from the benchmarks provide programmers with a basic intuitive grasp of the performance of a specific environment, when using C/C++.

The source code is provided to licensees of these guidelines and upon request from Plum Hall.

```
/* bench2 - driver for Plum Hall benchmarks
 * Thomas Plum, Plum Hall Inc, 609-927-3770, plumlumhall.com
 *
 * Written in "Typesafe C", the common subset of ANSI C and C++
 * Copyright (C) 1991, Plum Hall Inc.
 * Permission granted to reproduce for any purpose,
 * provided this copyright notice is preserved in the copy
 */
#include <stdio.h>
#include <stdlib.h>
#include <time.h>
/* put the following line in a separate source file,  f3.c ...
   void f3() { }
 */
void tabulate(void (*fn)(int, char*[]), char *s);
void benchreg(int ac, char *av[]);
void benchsho(int ac, char *av[]);
void benchlng(int ac, char *av[]);
void benchdbl(int ac, char *av[]);
void benchfn(int ac, char *av[]);

main(int argc, char *argv[])
    {
    char result[5][10];
    int i;

    if (argv[1][0] != '1')
        printf("argv[1] must be   1   !\n");
    if (argc < 3)
        {
        fprintf(stderr, "usage: bench2 1 'compiler-id'\n");
        exit(2);
        }
    tabulate(benchreg, result[0]);
    tabulate(benchsho, result[1]);
    tabulate(benchlng, result[2]);
    tabulate(benchfn,  result[3]);
    tabulate(benchdbl, result[4]);
    printf("\n\n");
    printf("%20.20s  %9s %9s %9s %9s %9s\n",
        "", "register", "auto", "auto", "function", "auto");
    printf("%20.20s  %9s %9s %9s %9s %9s\n",
        "", "int", "short", "long", "call+ret", "double");
    printf("%22.22s ",
        argv[2]);
    for (i = 0; i <= 4; ++i)
        printf("%9.9s ", result[i]);
    printf("\n");
    return 0;
    }
```

```
void tabulate(void (*fn)(int, char*[]), char *s)
    {
    static char arg1[20];
    static char *arga[3] = { "x", &arg1[0], 0 };
    double before, after, microsec;
    double resolution;
    long major, major_next;

    before = (double)clock();
    do  {
        after = (double)clock();
        } while (before == after);
    resolution = after - before;
    major_next = 1;
    do  {
        major = major_next;
        sprintf(arg1, "%ld", major);
        before = (double)clock();
        (*fn)(2, arga);
        after = (double)clock();
        major_next *= 10;
        } while (after-before < 100*resolution);
    microsec = 1e3 * (after - before) / CLOCKS_PER_SEC / major;
    sprintf(s, "%8.3g ", microsec);
    }

/* benchreg - benchmark for  register  integers
 * If machine traps overflow, use an  unsigned  type
 * Let  T  be the execution time in milliseconds
 * Then  average  time per operator  = T/major  usec
 * (Because the inner loop has exactly 1000 operations)
 */
void benchreg(int ac, char *av[])
    {
    register int a, b, c;
    long d, major;
    static int m[10] = {0};

    major = atol(av[1]);
    printf("executing %ld iterations\n", major);
    a = b = (av[1][0] - '0');
    for (d = 1; d <= major; ++d)
        /* inner loop executes 1000 selected operations */
        for (c = 1; c <= 40; ++c)
            {
            a = a+b+c; b = a>>1; a = b%10; m[a] = a; b = m[a]-b-c;
            a = b==c; b = a|c; a = !b; b = a+c; a = b>c;
            }
    printf("a=%d\n", a);
    }
```

```
/* benchsho - benchmark for  auto short  integers
 * If machine traps overflow, use an  unsigned  type
 */
void benchsho(int ac, char *av[])
    {
    auto short a, b, c;
    long d, major;
    static short m[10] = {0};

    major = atol(av[1]);
    printf("executing %ld iterations\n", major);
    a = b = (av[1][0] - '0');
    for (d = 1; d <= major; ++d)
        /* inner loop executes 1000 selected operations */
        for (c = 1; c <= 40; ++c)
            {
            a = a+b+c; b = a>>1; a = b%10; m[a] = a; b = m[a]-b-c;
            a = b==c; b = a|c; a = !b; b = a+c; a = b>c;
            }
    printf("a=%d\n", a);
    }
/* benchlng - benchmark for  auto long  integers
 * If machine traps overflow, use an  unsigned  type
 */
void benchlng(int ac, char *av[])
    {
    auto long a, b, c;
    long d, major;
    static long m[10] = {0};

    major = atol(av[1]);
    printf("executing %ld iterations\n", major);
    a = b = (av[1][0] - '0');
    for (d = 1; d <= major; ++d)
        /* inner loop executes 1000 selected operations */
        for (c = 1; c <= 40; ++c)
            {
            a = a+b+c; b = a>>1; a = b%10; m[a] = a; b = m[a]-b-c;
            a = b==c; b = a|c; a = !b; b = a+c; a = b>c;
            }
    printf("a=%d\n", a);
    }
```

```
/* benchdbl - benchmark for  double
 */
void benchdbl(int ac, char *av[])
    {
    auto double a, b, c;
    long d, major;

    major = atol(av[1]);
    printf("executing %ld iterations\n", major);
    a = b = (av[1][0] - '0');
    for (d = 1; d <= major; ++d)
        /* inner loop executes 1000 selected operations */
        for (c = 1; c <= 40; ++c)
            {
            a = a+b+c; b = a*2; a = b/10; a = -a; b = -a-b-c;
            a = b==c; b = a+c; a = !b; b = a+c; a = b>c;
            }
    printf("a=%d\n", a);
    }
/* benchfn - benchmark for function calls
 */
int dummy = 0;

extern void f3();  /* in separate source file */

void f2() { f3();f3();f3();f3();f3();f3();f3();f3();f3();f3();} /* 10 */
void f1() { f2();f2();f2();f2();f2();f2();f2();f2();f2();f2();} /* 10 */
void f0() { f1();f1();f1();f1();f1();f1();f1();f1();f1();} /* 9 */

void benchfn(int ac, char *av[])
    {
    long d, major;

    major = atol(av[1]);
    printf("executing %ld iterations\n", major);
    for (d = 1; d <= major; ++d)
        f0(); /* executes 1000 calls */
    printf("dummy=%d\n", dummy);
    }
```

Next, the files of the bench3 additional C++ benchmarks, starting with a
header:

```
// bench3h.h - define some virtual functions
class B
    {
    int i;
public:
    virtual void f() = 0;
    B(int ii) : i(ii) { }
    B() { }
    };
class D1 : public B
    {
public:
    void f();
    D1(int ii) : B(ii) { }
    D1() { }
    };
class D2 : public B
    {
public:
    void f();
    D2(int ii) : B(ii) { }
    D2() { }
    };
class D3 : public B
    {
public:
    void f();
    D3(int ii) : B(ii) { }
    D3() { }
    };
```

Next, the main program bench3.c:

```
/* bench3 - driver for Plum Hall C++ benchmarks
 * Thomas Plum, Plum Hall Inc, 609-927-3770, plumlumhall.com
 * Copyright (c) 1991, Plum Hall Inc
 * Permission is hereby granted to reproduce and use this program,
 * provided this copyright notice is preserved intact in all copies.
 */
/* link this program with separately-compiled  f4.c */
#include <stdio.h>
#include <stdlib.h>
#include <time.h>
void tabulate(void (*fn)(int, char*[]), char *s);
void benchkno(int ac, char *av[]);
void benchvir(int ac, char *av[]);
void benchcto(int ac, char *av[]);
```

```
main(int argc, char *argv[])
    {
    char result[5][10];
    int i;

    if (argv[1][0] != '1')
        printf("argv[1] must be   1   !\n");
    if (argc < 3)
        {
        fprintf(stderr, "usage: bench3  1  'compiler-id'\n");
        exit(2);
        }
    tabulate(benchkno, result[0]);
    tabulate(benchvir, result[1]);
    tabulate(benchcto, result[2]);
    printf("\n\n");
    printf("%20.20s  %9s %9s %9s\n", "", "virtual", "virtual", "plus");
    printf("%20.20s  %9s %9s %9s\n", "", "(known)", "(unknown)", "ctor/dtor");
    printf("%22.22s ", argv[2]);
    for (i = 0;  i <= 2;  ++i)
        printf("%9.9s ", result[i]);
    printf("\n");
    return 0;
    }
void tabulate(void (*fn)(int, char*[]), char *s)
    {
    static char arg1[20];
    static char *arga[3] = { "x", &arg1[0], 0 };
    double before, after, microsec;
    double resolution;
    long major, major_next;

    before = (double)clock();
    do {
        after = (double)clock();
        } while (before == after);
    resolution = after - before;
    major_next = 1;
    do {
        major = major_next;
        sprintf(arg1, "%ld", major);
        before = (double)clock();
        (*fn)(2, arga);
        after = (double)clock();
        major_next *= 10;
        } while (after-before < 100*resolution);
    microsec = 1e3 * (after - before) / CLOCKS_PER_SEC / major;
    sprintf(s, "%8.3g ", microsec);
    }
```

```
/* benchvir - benchmark for virtual (unknown) calls
 * "unknown", in that calling function doesn't know the type of call
 * Let  T  be the execution time in milliseconds
 * Then  average time per operator = T/major  usec
 * (Because the inner loop has exactly 1000 operations)
 */

#include "bench3h.h"

int dummy = 0;

void D1::f() { }
void D2::f() { }
void D3::f() { D2 id2 (0); }

D1 d1 (0);
D2 d2 (0);
D3 d3 (0);
B *p = &d1;

extern void f4();

void f0() { f4();f4();f4();f4();f4();f4();f4();f4();f4();f4();} /* 10 */

void benchvir(int ac, char *av[])
        {
        long d, major;

        major = atol(av[1]);
        printf("executing %ld iterations\n", major);
        for (d = 1; d <= major; ++d)
                f0(); /* executes 1000 calls */
        printf("dummy=%d\n", dummy);
        }

/* benchcto - benchmark for ctor/dtor  timing
 * adds one ctor/dtor pair to each  virtual-unknown call
 */
void benchcto(int ac, char *av[])
        {
        long d, major;

        p = &d3; // point to the fn with the ctor/dtor
        major = atol(av[1]);
        printf("executing %ld iterations\n", major);
        for (d = 1; d <= major; ++d)
                f0(); /* executes 1000 calls */
        printf("dummy=%d\n", dummy);
        }
```

```
/* benchkno - benchmark for  virtual (known)  calls
 * "known", in that calling function does know the type of call
 */

void f6() // 100 virtual calls
{
d2.f();d2.f();d2.f();d2.f();d2.f();d2.f();d2.f();d2.f();d2.f();d2.f();
d2.f();d2.f();d2.f();d2.f();d2.f();d2.f();d2.f();d2.f();d2.f();d2.f();
d2.f();d2.f();d2.f();d2.f();d2.f();d2.f();d2.f();d2.f();d2.f();d2.f();
d2.f();d2.f();d2.f();d2.f();d2.f();d2.f();d2.f();d2.f();d2.f();d2.f();
d2.f();d2.f();d2.f();d2.f();d2.f();d2.f();d2.f();d2.f();d2.f();d2.f();
d2.f();d2.f();d2.f();d2.f();d2.f();d2.f();d2.f();d2.f();d2.f();d2.f();
d2.f();d2.f();d2.f();d2.f();d2.f();d2.f();d2.f();d2.f();d2.f();d2.f();
d2.f();d2.f();d2.f();d2.f();d2.f();d2.f();d2.f();d2.f();d2.f();d2.f();
d2.f();d2.f();d2.f();d2.f();d2.f();d2.f();d2.f();d2.f();d2.f();d2.f();
d2.f();d2.f();d2.f();d2.f();d2.f();d2.f();d2.f();d2.f();d2.f();d2.f();
}
void f5() { f6();f6();f6();f6();f6();f6();f6();f6();f6();f6();} /* 10 */

void benchkno(int ac, char *av[])
	{
	long d, major;

	major = atol(av[1]);
	printf("executing %ld iterations\n", major);
	for (d = 1; d <= major; ++d)
		f5(); /* executes 1000 calls */
	printf("dummy=%d\n", dummy);
	}
```

Copyright © 1991, Thomas Plum and Dan Saks

```
// f4 - call the virtual functions (of unknown type)

#include "bench3h.h"

extern B *p;

void f4() // 100 virtual calls
{
p->f();p->f();p->f();p->f();p->f();p->f();p->f();p->f();p->f();p->f();
p->f();p->f();p->f();p->f();p->f();p->f();p->f();p->f();p->f();p->f();
p->f();p->f();p->f();p->f();p->f();p->f();p->f();p->f();p->f();p->f();
p->f();p->f();p->f();p->f();p->f();p->f();p->f();p->f();p->f();p->f();
p->f();p->f();p->f();p->f();p->f();p->f();p->f();p->f();p->f();p->f();
p->f();p->f();p->f();p->f();p->f();p->f();p->f();p->f();p->f();p->f();
p->f();p->f();p->f();p->f();p->f();p->f();p->f();p->f();p->f();p->f();
p->f();p->f();p->f();p->f();p->f();p->f();p->f();p->f();p->f();p->f();
p->f();p->f();p->f();p->f();p->f();p->f();p->f();p->f();p->f();p->f();
p->f();p->f();p->f();p->f();p->f();p->f();p->f();p->f();p->f();p->f();
}
```

[LOCAL NOTES]

TOPIC: 8.03 bib - bibliography

Ball, Michael S. 1989 February. Assignment and Initialization in C++. C++ Report. Vol 1. No 2. Pp 5-7.

Booch, Grady, and Michael Vilot. 1990 September. Evolving an object-oriented design. C++ Report. Vol 2. No 8. Pp 11-13.

Booch, Grady, and Michael Vilot. 1990 October. Inheritance relationships. C++ Report. Vol 2. No 9. Pp 8-11.

Booch, Grady. 1991. Object-Oriented Design. Benjamin/Cummings.

Cargill, Tom. 1990 Summer. Does Operator Overloading Help Systems Programmers. The C++ Journal. Pp 4-6.

Cargill, Tom. 1990 Fall. We Must Debate Multiple Inheritance. The C++ Journal. Pp 20-21.

Carolan, John. 1991 February. Building Bulletproof Classes. Workshop at Software Development '91 Conference."

Carroll, Martin. 1989 September. Profiling C++ Programs. C++ Report. Vol 1. No 8. Pp 7-11.

Carroll, Martin. 1990 September. Building Re-Useable C++ Components. C++ At Work.

Clamage, Steve. 1990 November 13. ANSI C Library Compatibility Issues. X3J16/90-0105. X3/CBEMA, Washington DC.

Coggins, James M. 1989 February. Is C++ Too Complex?. C++ Report. Vol 1. No 2. Pp 8-9.

Coggins, James M. 1989 April. Virtual Destruction. C++ Report. Vol 1. No 4. Pp 8-10.

Coggins, James M. 1989 May. Virtual Destruction: Part 2. C++ Report. Vol 1. No 5. Pp 8-10.

Coggins, James M. 1989 October. Return Types of Member Functions. C++ Report. Vol 1. No 9. Pp 11-13.

Coggins, James M. 1989 November/December. Return Types of Member Functions. C++ Report. Vol 1. No 10. Pp 11-14.

Coggins, James M. 1990 April. Real Benefits vs. Intellectual Fads. C++ Report. Vol 2. No 4. Pp 11-13.

Coggins, James M. 1990 Summer. Designing C++ Libraries. The C++ Journal. Pp 25-32.

Coggins, James M. 1990 October. Copying: not as easy as it sounds. C++ Report. Vol 2. No 9. Pp 12-14.

Coggins, James M. and Gregory Bollella. 1989 June. Managing C++ Libraries. SIGPLAN Notices. Vol 24. No 6. Pp 37-48.

Dearle, Fergal. 1990 Summer. Designing Portable Application Frameworks for C++. Pp 55-59.

Dewhurst, Stephen C. and Kathy T. Stark. 1989. Programming in C++. Prentice-Hall.

Eckel, Bruce. 1989. Using C++. Osborne McGraw-Hill.

Ellis, Margaret A. and Bjarne Stroustrup. 1990. The Annotated C++ Reference Manual. Addison-Wesley.

Fontana, Mary, LaMott Oren, and Martin Neath. 1990. A Portable Implementation of Paramaterized Templates Using a Sophisticated C++ Macro Facility. C++ at Work-'90 Conference Proceedings. Pp 73-82.

Gorlen, Keith E. 1990 Fall. Libraries in C++. The C++ Journal. Pp 54-58.

Gorlen, Keith E., Sanford M. Orlow, and Perry S. Plexico. 1990. Data Abstraction and Object-Oriented Programming in C++. John Wiley & Sons.

Hansen, Tony L. 1990. The C++ Answer Book. Addison-Wesley.

Jordan, David. 1990 September. Implementation Benefits of C++ Language Mechanisms. Communications of the ACM. Vol 33. No 9. Pp 61-64.

Koenig, Andrew and Bjarne Stroustrup. 1989 August/September. C++: As Close as Possible to C -- But No Closer. C++ Report.

Koenig, Andrew. 1990 Summer. Applicators, Manipulators, & Function Objects. The C++ Journal.

Lippman, Stanley B. 1989 (Corrected 1990). C++ Primer. Addison-Wesley.

Lippman, Stanley B. 1990 Summer. C++: How Release 2.0 Differs from Release 1.2. The C++ Journal. Pp 7-13.

Lippman, Stanley B. 1990 Fall. Nested Types in C++. The C++ Journal. Pp 31-33.

Mancl, Dennis. 1989 September. C++ Software Metrics. C++ At Work.

Miller, William M. 1990 Summer. ANSI Update. The C++ Journal. Pp 34-42

Miller, William M. 1990 Fall. ANSI Update. The C++ Journal. Pp 34-42.

Plum, Thomas. 1989. C Programming Guidelines (Second Edition). Plum Hall.

Plum, Thomas. 1985. Reliable Data Structures in C. Plum Hall.

Plum, Thomas. 1989. Learning to Program in C (Second Edition). Plum Hall.

Saks, Dan. 1991 January. Paving the Migration Path. The C Users Journal. Vol 9. No 1. Pp 87-92.

Saks, Dan. 1991 March. Writing Your First Class. The C Users Journal. Vol 9. No 3. Pp 115-122.

Schwarz, Jerry. 1989 February. Initializing Static Variables in C++ Libraries. C++ Report. Vol 1. No 2. Pp 1-4.

Schwarz, Jerry. 1990 Fall. C++ is not an Object-Oriented Language. The C++ Journal. Pp 3-6.

Schwarz, Jerry. 1991 February 8. Mixed C and C++ Environments. X3J16/91-0011. X3/CBEMA Washington DC.

Stroustrup, Bjarne. 1986. The C++ Programming Language. Addison-Wesley.

Tiemann, Michael. 1989 July/August. Objects as Return Values. C++ Report. Vol 1. No 7. Pp 8-9.

Wegner, Peter. 1990 August. Concepts and Paradigms of Object-Oriented Programming. OOPS Messenger.

Wirfs-Brock, Rebecca J., and Ralph E. Johnson. 1990 September. Surveying Current Research in Object-Oriented Design. Communications of the ACM. Vol 33. No 9. Pp 104-124.

INDEX

In this index, items are identified by both page number and section number. For example, the citation "80(1.23)" refers to page 80, in section 1.23. The format of the index and the bibliography is intentionally simplified to maximize compatibility between the printed and machine-readable editions.

0, null-pointer constant   80(1.23)
31-character names   176(5.01)
a[*] (the entire array a, for emphasis)   65(1.16)
a[*] => sorted (notation indicating that a[*] is now sorted)   65(1.16)
abbreviations   64(1.16)
abstract-const   48(1.11)
abstract data type   20(1.01)
access control   12(0.02), 210(6.08), 212(6.09)
access rules   58(1.14)
access specifier   55(1.13)
accessor function   20(1.01), 212(6.09)
ADT, abstract data type   20(1.01), 212(6.09)
advantages of standards: efficiency   98(2.03), 124(3.04), 134(4.02), 152(4.10), 160(4.14), 177(5.01), 222(6.13), 250(8.02)
advantages of standards: portability   18(0.04), 28(1.04), 68(1.17), 70(1.18), 72(1.19), 74(1.20), 76(1.21), 80(1.23), 84(1.25), 92(2.02), 104(2.06), 108(2.08), 110(2.09), 114(2.11), 116(3.01), 138(4.04), 162(4.15), 168(4.18), 186(5.04), 196(6.03), 226(6.15), 228(7.01), 232(7.02), 240(7.05), 242(7.06)
advantages of standards: readability   20(1.01), 66(1.16), 68(1.17), 70(1.18), 92(2.02), 116(3.01), 120(3.03), 124(3.04), 136(4.03), 140(4.05), 160(4.14), 168(4.18), 183(5.03), 218(6.11), 222(6.13)
advantages of standards: reliability   20(1.01), 32(1.06), 52(1.12), 60(1.15), 66(1.16), 68(1.17), 70(1.18), 82(1.24), 88(2.01), 98(2.03), 100(2.04), 104(2.06), 120(3.03), 126(3.05), 134(4.02), 138(4.04), 140(4.05), 166(4.17), 170(4.19), 183(5.03), 192(6.02), 204(6.06), 208(6.07), 212(6.09), 220(6.12), 222(6.13), 224(6.14), 226(6.15), 240(7.05)
aggregate initializer, lexical rules   180(5.03)
aggregate initializers   176(5.01)
a[i:j] (the subarray a[i] through a[j])   65(1.16)
allocation integrity   82(1.24)
allowable dependencies on evaluation order   104(2.06)
anachronisms   228(7.01)
and, proposed new keyword   236(7.04)
ANSI   229(7.01)
architectural issues in code re-use   188(6.01)
arguments   156(4.12)
arguments, variable number of   168(4.18)
array bounds   70(1.18)
array of derived class objects   208(6.07)
arrays   136(4.03)
asm, new keyword   236(7.04)
assertions   66(1.16)

aggregate initializer, lexical rules   180(5.03)
aggregate initializers   176(5.01)
a[i:j] (the subarray a[i] through a[j])   65(1.16)
allocation integrity   82(1.24)
allowable dependencies on evaluation order   104(2.06)
anachronisms   228(7.01)
and, proposed new keyword   236(7.04)
ANSI   229(7.01)
architectural issues in code re-use   188(6.01)
arguments   156(4.12)
arguments, variable number of   168(4.18)
array bounds   70(1.18)
array of derived class objects   208(6.07)
arrays   136(4.03)
asm, new keyword   236(7.04)
assertions   66(1.16)
assignment   44(1.10), 92(2.02)
assignment operator   21(1.01)
AT&T C++ Release 2.1   229(7.01)
automatic variable, taking address of   82(1.24)
avoiding changes to derived classes   210(6.08)
base class   132(4.01), 204(6.06), 208(6.07), 210(6.08)
"Better C"   13(0.02)
bibliography   260(8.03)
binary data, and portability   74(1.20)
binary operator   54(1.13), 92(2.02)
binding time, and segregation of environment-specific code   196(6.03)
bitand, proposed new keyword   236(7.04)
bitcompl, proposed new keyword   236(7.04)
bit-fields   84(1.25)
bit-not, and portable masks   72(1.19)
bitor, proposed new keyword   236(7.04)
bits(n) property (used for bitwise operations on n bits)   65(1.16)
bitwise operators   106(2.07)
bitxor, proposed new keyword   236(7.04)
BNF (Backus Normal Form, or Backus Naur Form)   128(3.06)
bool   183(5.03)
bool defined-type   68(1.17), 173(4.20)
bool property (tested for either false (zero) or true (non-zero))   65(1.16)
bracing styles   180(5.03)
break   124(3.04)
BUFSIZ   70(1.18)
byte ordering   74(1.20)
C   232(7.02)
C versus C++   234(7.03)
cast   30(1.05), 48(1.11), 49(1.11), 100(2.04), 102(2.05), 228(7.01)
cast, pointer   74(1.20)
casting objects   102(2.05)
catch   229(7.01)
catch, new keyword   236(7.04)
cerr   162(4.15)
char   72(1.19)
character constants   76(1.21)
character tests   114(2.11)
Cheshire Cat technique   214(6.10)
choice (syntax and control structure)   128(3.06)
choosing variable names   64(1.16)
cin   162(4.15)

concrete-const   48(1.11)
concrete const vs. abstract const   48(1.11)
conditional compilation   26(1.03)
configuration file, for environment-specific values   197(6.03)
const   28(1.04), 48(1.11), 102(2.05)
const *, for unmodified arguments   134(4.02)
const &, for unmodified arguments   134(4.02)
const definition   130(4.01)
const, explicit storage-class, in Typesafe C   237(7.04)
const member function   48(1.11), 52(1.12)
const member functions   52(1.12)
const static data member   229(7.01)
constant, manifest   70(1.18)
constructor   26(1.03), 41(1.09), 48(1.11), 228(7.01)
container class   32(1.06), 36(1.07), 40(1.09), 60(1.15)
contents of local standard headers   172(4.20)
context data, handled by global data   156(4.12)
continue   126(3.05)
control structures, lexical rules   180(5.03)
conversion operator   36(1.07)
conversions and overflow   112(2.10)
conversions, pointer   80(1.23)
COOL preprocessor   242(7.06)
copy constructor   21(1.01), 32(1.06)
copying   95(2.02)
coupling   55(1.13), 156(4.12), 210(6.08), 212(6.09)
cout   162(4.15)
__cplusplus, seldom needed in Typesafe C   238(7.04)
<ctype.h>   114(2.11)
dangling pointer   88(2.01)
dangling pointers   82(1.24)
dangling references   38(1.08), 88(2.01)
data abstraction   12(0.02)
data pointer   30(1.05)
debugging   26(1.03), 98(2.03)
declarations   176(5.01)
decrement   110(2.09)
de-facto standard for C++   18(0.04)
default   124(3.04)
default arguments   136(4.03), 228(7.01)
default assignment   32(1.06), 92(2.02)
default constructor   21(1.01), 44(1.10), 136(4.03), 228(7.01)
defensive programming   224(6.14)
#define   148(4.08)
defined-types   68(1.17)
definitions, file-level   177(5.01)
delete   58(1.14), 82(1.24), 98(2.03)
delete, lexical rules   178(5.02)
delete, new keyword   236(7.04)
derived class   12(0.02), 60(1.15), 102(2.05), 132(4.01), 204(6.06), 208(6.07), 210(6.08),
   242(7.06)
design   212(6.09)
designing with loop invariants   120(3.03)
destructor   21(1.01), 26(1.03), 48(1.11), 215(6.10), 232(7.02)
DIM   175(4.20)
discriminated union   204(6.06)
documentation   21(1.01), 32(1.06)
dollars property (represents currency in dollars)   65(1.16)

defensive programming   224(6.14)
#define   148(4.08)
defined-types   68(1.17)
definitions, file-level   177(5.01)
delete   58(1.14), 82(1.24), 98(2.03)
delete, lexical rules   178(5.02)
delete, new keyword   236(7.04)
derived class   12(0.02), 60(1.15), 102(2.05), 132(4.01), 204(6.06), 208(6.07), 210(6.08),
    242(7.06)
design   212(6.09)
designing with loop invariants   120(3.03)
destructor   21(1.01), 26(1.03), 48(1.11), 215(6.10), 232(7.02)
DIM   175(4.20)
discriminated union   204(6.06)
documentation   21(1.01), 32(1.06)
dollars property (represents currency in dollars)   65(1.16)
domain of exceptions to data invariant   64(1.16)
domain of exceptions to loop invariant   120(3.03)
do-while   126(3.05)
dynamics of temporaries   88(2.01)
effects of constructors and destructors   26(1.03)
efficiency   45(1.10), 95(2.02), 98(2.03), 124(3.04), 134(4.02), 152(4.10), 160(4.14),
    177(5.01), 200(6.05), 204(6.06), 215(6.10), 222(6.13), 250(8.02)
efficiency of virtual function   55(1.13)
Efficient C (EFC)   200(6.05)
element of vector   33(1.06)
else-if   124(3.04)
embedded assignment   183(5.03)
encapsulated data type (synonym for abstract data type)   20(1.01)
encapsulation   12(0.02)
enum   28(1.04)
enumeration   204(6.06)
enumeration type   228(7.01)
enumeration types, keep distinct in Typesafe C   237(7.04)
enumerator   204(6.06)
environ   186(5.04)
environmental data, handled by global data   156(4.12)
EOF   70(1.18)
errno   112(2.10)
error-handling   192(6.02)
evaluation order   104(2.06)
exception handling   12(0.02)
exceptions   229(7.01)
exceptions, allowed if documented   11(0.01)
excess generality   24(1.02)
exit   70(1.18)
EXIT_FAILURE   70(1.18)
explicit initializer   44(1.10)
extern and declarations   177(5.01)
extern declaration   130(4.01)
extern C, and Typesafe C   237(7.04)
external declarations   186(5.04)
FALSE   175(4.20)
fclose   82(1.24)
fclose, and defensive programming   224(6.14)
ferror   82(1.24)
ferror, and defensive programming   224(6.14)
fflush, and defensive programming   224(6.14)

function definition   228(7.01)
function definitions   186(5.04)
function name overloading   12(0.02)
function pointer   30(1.05)
function returning reference   38(1.08)
functional cohesiveness   158(4.13)
functions, lexical rules   186(5.04)
functions of a variable number of arguments   168(4.18)
functions, suggested size   164(4.16)
general expression   27(1.03)
general-purpose functions, and file structure   160(4.14)
generic class   60(1.15)
generic function   60(1.15)
generic pointer (void *)   78(1.22)
generic.h   242(7.06)
''get'' function (accessor)   20(1.01)
getenv, to access environment-specific values   197(6.03)
global linkage   156(4.12)
global name   28(1.04)
global name conflicts   28(1.04), 40(1.09), 58(1.14)
global non-member data   28(1.04)
goto   126(3.05)
guideline (recommended practice)   11(0.01)
has-a relationships   40(1.09)
header file   130(4.01)
headers   144(4.06), 152(4.10), 172(4.20)
heterogeneous container   62(1.15), 242(7.06)
high precedence   179(5.02)
homogeneous container   62(1.15)
#if 0, for commenting-out sections of code   218(6.11)
#ifdef, to provide test driver   160(4.14)
if-else   126(3.05)
#ifndef, to prevent multiple inclusion   152(4.10)
imod   112(2.10), 173(4.20)
#include   148(4.08)
incomplete type   215(6.10)
increment   110(2.09)
index_t   172(4.20)
inheritance   12(0.02), 102(2.05), 212(6.09)
inherited function   54(1.13)
initialization   26(1.03), 95(2.02)
initialization of global objects   138(4.04)
initialization, static storage   138(4.04)
initializer   44(1.10), 49(1.11)
initializer list   228(7.01)
initializers   176(5.01)
initializers, not allowed in headers   154(4.11)
inline, new keyword   236(7.04)
inline function   12(0.02), 28(1.04), 62(1.15), 130(4.01), 136(4.03)
in-only pointers   170(4.19)
in-only references   170(4.19)
in-out pointers   170(4.19)
in-out references   170(4.19)
input   26(1.03)
Instant-C(tm)   142(4.05)
int and portability   68(1.17)
internal function   54(1.13), 212(6.09)
internal representation of class   36(1.07)

initialization, static storage   138(4.04)
initializer   44(1.10), 49(1.11)
initializer list   228(7.01)
initializers   176(5.01)
initializers, not allowed in headers   154(4.11)
inline, new keyword   236(7.04)
inline function   12(0.02), 28(1.04), 62(1.15), 130(4.01), 136(4.03)
in-only pointers   170(4.19)
in-only references   170(4.19)
in-out pointers   170(4.19)
in-out references   170(4.19)
input   26(1.03)
Instant-C(tm)   142(4.05)
int and portability   68(1.17)
internal function   54(1.13), 212(6.09)
internal representation of class   36(1.07)
interrupts, in mixed C/C++   240(7.05)
InterViews 3.0 library   29(1.04)
intuitive properties, of overloaded operators   90(2.02)
invariant condition of a loop   120(3.03)
invariant property of variable   64(1.16)
iostream.h   232(7.02)
ISO/IEC 9899 (ISO C Standard)   234(7.03)
iterators   40(1.09)
iterators, prefer next to ()   91(2.02)
just-a-struct   24(1.02), 49(1.11), 212(6.09), 232(7.02)
just-a-struct (not an ADT)   24(1.02)
keep casts significant   100(2.04)
Kernighan, Brian   180(5.03)
keywords, followed by one space   179(5.02)
keywords, new in C++   236(7.04)
ldouble defined-type   68(1.17)
left operand   54(1.13)
levels of use   12(0.02), 24(1.02), 204(6.06)
lexical rules for control structure   180(5.03)
lexical rules for functions   186(5.04)
lexical rules for operators   178(5.02)
lexical rules for variables   176(5.01)
library, and portability   162(4.15)
library functions, and file structure   160(4.14)
lifetime of referenced object   32(1.06)
link error   92(2.02)
linkers   176(5.01)
lint   100(2.04)
{lo, b:c, hi} property (range of values lo, b through c, and hi)   65(1.16)
local standard headers   172(4.20)
local static objects   44(1.10)
local.h   144(4.06), 174(4.20)
{lo:hi} property (range of values from lo to hi)   65(1.16)
{>lo:<hi} property (range of values greater than lo and less than hi)   65(1.16)
long   72(1.19)
longjmp   232(7.02)
low precedence   179(5.02)
lower-case names, for functions and protected macros   166(4.17)
lvalue   33(1.06)
machine-readable version of Guidelines   6
macro   28(1.04), 62(1.15)
magic numbers   71(1.18)

methods of coupling modules together   156(4.12)
migrating from C to C++   234(7.03)
minimizing use of preprocessor   140(4.05)
mixing C and C++ code   240(7.05)
mktemp   86(1.26)
modifiability   70(1.18)
multi-character constants   76(1.21)
multiple-choice constructs   124(3.04)
mutator function   20(1.01), 212(6.09)
N+1/2 - time loop   118(3.02)
N+1/4 - time loop   118(3.02)
name conflict, global   28(1.04), 40(1.09), 58(1.14)
names   64(1.16), 176(5.01)
names, for functions and macros   166(4.17)
NAM_LEN_EXTERNAL   172(4.20), 176(5.01)
nested headers   152(4.10)
nested types   40(1.09), 41(1.09), 228(7.01)
nesting of comments (not in Standard C)   218(6.11)
new   58(1.14), 98(2.03), 228(7.01)
new, lexical rules   178(5.02)
new, new keyword   236(7.04)
niladic functions, in Typesafe C   237(7.04)
NO   175(4.20)
no initializations in headers   154(4.11)
non-inline function   130(4.01)
non-member function   28(1.04)
non-member static data   216(6.10)
nul (the char value ' ')   65(1.16)
NULL   30(1.05), 70(1.18), 232(7.02)
NULL, not for pointer-to-function   78(1.22)
null pointer   30(1.05), 38(1.08)
null pointer constant   30(1.05)
null statement, on its own line   183(5.03)
object declaration and initialization   44(1.10)
object file   130(4.01)
object library   130(4.01)
Object-Based C++   12(0.02), 20(1.01), 204(6.06)
object-based programming   12(0.02), 28(1.04)
object-oriented design   210(6.08)
object-oriented programming   12(0.02), 28(1.04)
offsetof   84(1.25), 232(7.02)
offsets, of structure members   84(1.25)
one-too-far values, and ranges   65(1.16)
operator[]   32(1.06)
operator--   228(7.01)
operator++   228(7.01)
operator, new keyword   236(7.04)
operator overloading   12(0.02)
or, proposed new keyword   236(7.04)
order of evaluation   104(2.06)
order of operations   95(2.02)
order of side effects   110(2.09)
order of static initialization   26(1.03)
out-of-bounds data (must not blow up)   224(6.14)
out-only pointers   170(4.19)
out-only references   170(4.19)
output   26(1.03)
overflow   112(2.10)

one-too-far values, and ranges   65(1.16)
operator[]   32(1.06)
operator--   228(7.01)
operator++   228(7.01)
operator, new keyword   236(7.04)
operator overloading   12(0.02)
or, proposed new keyword   236(7.04)
order of evaluation   104(2.06)
order of operations   95(2.02)
order of side effects   110(2.09)
order of static initialization   26(1.03)
out-of-bounds data (must not blow up)   224(6.14)
out-only pointers   170(4.19)
out-only references   170(4.19)
output   26(1.03)
overflow   112(2.10)
overload   228(7.01)
overloaded binary operator   92(2.02)
overloaded function   136(4.03)
overloaded operators, intuitive properties of   90(2.02)
overloaded operators, precedence   91(2.02)
overloading   90(2.02)
overloading new and delete   98(2.03)
p[*] (the entire array accessed through p)   65(1.16)
paradigm shift   13(0.02)
paragraph (logical grouping of statements)   218(6.11)
parameter   32(1.06)
parameter, pointer-to-class-object   170(4.19)
parameterized types   60(1.15), 242(7.06)
parentheses   106(2.07), 178(5.02)
pass-through parameters   156(4.12)
pennies property (represents currency in pennies)   65(1.16)
performance analysis   26(1.03)
placement of declarations   44(1.10)
placement syntax   98(2.03), 228(7.01)
pointer   36(1.07), 38(1.08), 102(2.05), 208(6.07)
pointer and reference parameters   170(4.19)
pointer cast   74(1.20)
pointer conversions   80(1.23)
pointer into object   36(1.07)
pointer parameters, using * or []   170(4.19)
pointer to function   102(2.05), 228(7.01)
pointer to member function   228(7.01)
pointer types   78(1.22)
pointers-to-functions   78(1.22)
pointer-to-const, for unmodified arguments   134(4.02)
pointer-to-class-object parameter   170(4.19)
polymorphism   12(0.02), 60(1.15), 242(7.06)
portability   18(0.04), 28(1.04), 41(1.09), 49(1.11), 50(1.11), 68(1.17), 70(1.18), 72(1.19),
    74(1.20), 76(1.21), 80(1.23), 84(1.25), 92(2.02), 102(2.05), 104(2.06), 108(2.08),
    110(2.09), 114(2.11), 116(3.01), 138(4.04), 162(4.15), 168(4.18), 186(5.04), 196(6.03),
    226(6.15), 228(7.01), 232(7.02), 240(7.05), 242(7.06)
portability and intentional non-portability   196(6.03)
portdefs.h   172(4.20)
precedence   106(2.07)
precedence, and overloaded operators   91(2.02)
precedence levels   179(5.02)
prefix   28(1.04)

protected member function   212(6.09)
protected members   212(6.09)
prototypes, in Typesafe C   237(7.04)
pseudo-code   218(6.11)
public, new keyword   236(7.04)
public data member   20(1.01), 212(6.09)
public derivation   212(6.09)
public member function, and defensive programming   224(6.14)
put includes at head of file   148(4.08)
putenv   186(5.04)
readability   20(1.01), 66(1.16), 68(1.17), 70(1.18), 92(2.02), 116(3.01), 120(3.03),
   124(3.04), 136(4.03), 140(4.05), 160(4.14), 168(4.18), 183(5.03), 218(6.11), 222(6.13)
readonly memory   48(1.11)
reference   12(0.02), 32(1.06), 38(1.08), 102(2.05)
reference-to-const, for unmodified arguments   134(4.02)
referencing unmodified arguments   134(4.02)
referencing-declarations   177(5.01)
register declarations   68(1.17), 176(5.01)
relational operators, not defaulting zero   183(5.03)
reliability   20(1.01), 32(1.06), 52(1.12), 60(1.15), 66(1.16), 68(1.17), 70(1.18), 82(1.24),
   88(2.01), 98(2.03), 100(2.04), 104(2.06), 120(3.03), 126(3.05), 134(4.02), 138(4.04),
   140(4.05), 166(4.17), 170(4.19), 183(5.03), 192(6.02), 204(6.06), 208(6.07), 212(6.09),
   220(6.12), 222(6.13), 224(6.14), 226(6.15), 240(7.05)
Reliable Data Structures in C (RDS)   82(1.24)
renaming macro   29(1.04)
repetition (syntax and control structure)   128(3.06)
reserved words (names of Standard Library functions)   160(4.14)
resource management   26(1.03)
restrictions on control structures   126(3.05)
return type   32(1.06)
review, first-order correctness   244(8.01)
reviews   222(6.13)
right-shift and unsigned data   108(2.08)
Ritchie, Dennis   180(5.03)
ROM   48(1.11)
schar defined-type   68(1.17), 173(4.20)
scope of loop variable   116(3.01)
scope rules   41(1.09)
SEEK_CUR   70(1.18)
SEEK_END   70(1.18)
SEEK_SET   70(1.18)
sequence points   110(2.09)
sequence (syntax and control structure)   128(3.06)
"set" function (mutator)   20(1.01)
setjmp   232(7.02)
shared data   58(1.14)
short   72(1.19)
side effects   110(2.09), 118(3.02)
side-effects   26(1.03)
signal function, in mixed C/C++   240(7.05)
simple benchmark programs   250(8.02)
simplicity of design and implementation   226(6.15)
size of functions   164(4.16)
size of source files   146(4.07)
sizeof   236(7.04)
sizes for data   72(1.19)
size_t defined-type   68(1.17)
smart pointer   32(1.06)

sequence (syntax and control structure)   128(3.06)
"set" function (mutator)   20(1.01)
setjmp   232(7.02)
shared data   58(1.14)
short   72(1.19)
side effects   110(2.09), 118(3.02)
side-effects   26(1.03)
signal function, in mixed C/C++   240(7.05)
simple benchmark programs   250(8.02)
simplicity of design and implementation   226(6.15)
size of functions   164(4.16)
size of source files   146(4.07)
sizeof   236(7.04)
sizes for data   72(1.19)
size_t defined-type   68(1.17)
smart pointer   32(1.06)
source file   130(4.01)
source file, and defensive programming   224(6.14)
source files (size limit)   146(4.07)
spaces, and lexical rules for operators   178(5.02)
specifications   220(6.12)
stack space   215(6.10)
standard compile-time flags   150(4.09)
standard defined-types   68(1.17)
standard (mandatory practice)   11(0.01)
standards and guidelines   11(0.01)
static const data member   229(7.01)
static data member initializer   130(4.01)
static data members   26(1.03), 28(1.04), 58(1.14), 228(7.01)
static initializer   27(1.03)
static member initializer   26(1.03)
static non-member data   28(1.04)
static non-member function   28(1.04)
static storage, initialization   138(4.04)
static typing   60(1.15), 242(7.06)
<stdarg.h>   168(4.18)
stderr   162(4.15)
STDERR   172(4.20)
stdin   162(4.15)
STDIN   172(4.20)
<stdio.h>   70(1.18)
stdio.h   232(7.02)
stdout   162(4.15)
STDOUT   172(4.20)
stream.h   232(7.02)
STRICTEST_ALIGNMENT   173(4.20)
string property (contains a null-terminator)   65(1.16)
string literals   86(1.26)
struct   20(1.01), 24(1.02)
struct, just-a-struct   24(1.02)
structures   84(1.25)
subdirectory   132(4.01)
sub-object   102(2.05)
subscript limits   70(1.18)
subtraction of unsigned int's   112(2.10)
suggested size of functions   164(4.16)
suggested use of comments   218(6.11)
switch   124(3.04)

throw, new keyword   236(7.04)
TRUE   175(4.20)
truncation with masks not casts   72(1.19)
try   229(7.01)
try, new keyword   236(7.04)
TRYMAIN   160(4.14)
type field   204(6.06)
type name   41(1.09)
typedef of tag names, in Typesafe C   236(7.04)
Typesafe C (common subset of C and C++)   12(0.02), 48(1.11), 234(7.03), 236(7.04)
Typesafe C, when to use   236(7.04)
typical picture of a loop   120(3.03)
uchar defined-type   68(1.17), 173(4.20)
uint defined-type   68(1.17), 173(4.20)
ulong defined-type   68(1.17), 173(4.20)
unambiguous conversion   102(2.05)
unchecked argument   30(1.05)
#undef   29(1.04)
underscore, double, reserved in names   236(7.04)
uniform naming schemes   40(1.09)
units of measure (in property comments)   65(1.16)
UNIX   144(4.06), 186(5.04)
unprotected macro   62(1.15)
unprotected macros, distinct from functions   166(4.17)
upper-case names, for unprotected macros   166(4.17)
use of portable library   162(4.15)
use of references   32(1.06)
user-defined conversion   54(1.13)
ushort defined-type   68(1.17), 173(4.20)
variable number of function arguments   168(4.18)
variable-length argument list   30(1.05)
variable-size class   92(2.02)
variadic function   168(4.18)
verb+object comment   218(6.11)
verb+object description (test for cohesiveness)   158(4.13)
versions of C++   228(7.01)
virtual, new keyword   236(7.04)
virtual base class   102(2.05)
virtual destructors   208(6.07)
virtual function   204(6.06)
virtual functions   12(0.02), 54(1.13), 60(1.15), 102(2.05), 204(6.06), 242(7.06)
void *   102(2.05), 242(7.06)
void *, containers of   60(1.15)
void * (generic pointer)   78(1.22)
void * pointers, and Typesafe C   238(7.04)
(void) casts, to be avoided   224(6.14)
void in prototypes, in Typesafe C   237(7.04)
volatile   229(7.01)
walkthrough   222(6.13), 244(8.01)
well-defined object (all members have defining properties)   66(1.16)
when to use C, when to use C++   234(7.03)
which design methods to use   16(0.03)
while   118(3.02)
while   126(3.05)
word and byte size   72(1.19)
writing macros   166(4.17)
X3.159-1989 (ANSI C Standard)   234(7.03)
X3J16   229(7.01)

void *, containers of   60(1.15)
void * (generic pointer)   78(1.22)
void * pointers, and Typesafe C   238(7.04)
(void) casts, to be avoided   224(6.14)
void in prototypes, in Typesafe C   237(7.04)
volatile   229(7.01)
walkthrough   222(6.13), 244(8.01)
well-defined object (all members have defining properties)   66(1.16)
when to use C, when to use C++   234(7.03)
which design methods to use   16(0.03)
while   118(3.02)
while   126(3.05)
word and byte size   72(1.19)
writing macros   166(4.17)
X3.159-1989 (ANSI C Standard)   234(7.03)
X3J16   229(7.01)
YES   175(4.20)
zero   30(1.05)
zero-initialized structures   66(1.16)

PLUM HALL PRODUCTS

Please give Plum Hall a call or an e-mail for information on the following products and services:

License for Machine-Readable C++ Programming Guidelines

Your entire organization, or one specific site, can license the reproduction of this *C++ Programming Guidelines* book. You can use it as the starting point for your own in-house programming standard, modifying, adding, and deleting as your group desires. You can then distribute it internally in printed form or on-line.

Suite++™: The Plum Hall Validation Suite for C++

Source code of test cases comparing compiler behavior to the (draft) ANSI/ISO C++ standard. Includes positive tests (for required behavior) and negative tests (for production of diagnostic messages).

The Plum Hall Validation Suite for C

The authoritative test suite for ANSI/ISO C, with positive and negative tests for all requirements of the ANSI/ISO C Standard. Used for accredited certification by the European Compiler Testing Service (British Standards Institution, AFNOR, IMQ).

C Programming Guidelines Machine-Readable

The Plum Hall textbook *C Programming Guidelines* is licensed by over 100 companies world-wide as the basis for their internal C programming standard.

P. J. Plauger's "Standard C Library"

P. J. Plauger's best-selling textbook *The Standard C Library* (published by Prentice-Hall) contains full source code for a library conforming to the ANSI/ISO C Standard. Plum Hall serves as the licensing agency for organizations who wish to distribute this library as part of their C or C++ implementations.

PLUM HALL INC
+1-609-927-3770
plum@plumhall.com

Get FREE information on our newest programming books!

If you would like to receive information on the most advanced programming books published, simply fill out this card and mail it to:

R&D Publications
1601 West 23rd Street, Suite 200
P.O. Box 3127
Lawrence, KS 66046-0127

Name _____

Job Title _____

Address _____

City/State/Zip _____

Telephone Number _____

Please take a moment to answer the following questions. This information will be used to help us publish the types of books you need most. It will also help us find the best way to make these books available to you. Thanks for your help.

I'm particularly interested in the following:
(please check all that apply)

___ C++   ___ TurboC/C++   ___ MS/DOS internals
___ ANSI/Standard C   ___ Windows   ___ Graphics
___ UNIX   ___ Object Oriented Programs   ___ other _____

The operating system I work on is:

___ MVS   ___ UNIX   ___ OS/2
___ VMS   ___ Xenix   ___ OS/400
___ MS-DOS   ___ Apple/Mac ___ other _____

I purchased this book from a:

___ bookstore   ___ mailing
___ catalog   ___ other _____
___ advertisement

I read the following magazines:

___ The C++ Journal   ___ C Gazette   ___ C Users Journal
___ Computer Language   ___ Dr. Dobbs   ___ Embedded Sys Programming
___ Microsoft Sys Journal ___ PC Techniques ___ Windows/DOS Developer's Journal
___ Programmer's Journal ___ Windows OS/2   ___ other _____

Please fold on the dotted line and seal loose edge with tape (Do not staple) before mailing this card.

Fold here before mailing —